ENGAGING
SPEAKERS
VOICES OF TRUTH

Presented by

Engaging Speakers

www.EngagingSpeakers.com

For more information, contact:
Engaging Speakers
Info@EngagingSpeakers.com
www.EngagingSpeakers.com

Publisher: DPWN Publishing
1879 N. Neltnor Blvd. #316, West Chicago, IL 60185
www.OurDPWN.com

Printed in the United States of America

ISBN: 978-1-939794-23-9

ENGAGING SPEAKERS

Dedication

This book is dedicated to the founder of Engaging Speakers, Gail Brown, who has a heart of gold and a huge passion for helping entrepreneurs. It is my great honor to bring her vision for Engaging Speakers to life as the premier global coaching company teaching entrepreneurs how to speak their way to more business. It is also dedicated to Louie Sharp, who has been beside me since the very beginning and is always happy to help and support the organization in any way he can.

A special dedication to my business partner, my confidant, my encourager, my systems girl, my spiritual sister, and one of my best friends in life, Rachelle Ferguson. Thank you, Rachelle, for all you have contributed to Engaging Speakers. The organization would not be what it is today, without all the time and talents you have invested.

"The two most important days in your life are the day you are born and the day you find out why."

—Mark Twain

Introduction

Voices of Truth is a compilation of Engaging Speakers sharing their stories of impact. They each started their businesses because they have a desire to make an impact in the world with their message. For these authors and for you, our readers, stories have the power to change us, especially true stories.

Stories inspire us. Stories tap into our emotions. Stories build the belief that we can overcome. Stories teach us lessons on life. Stories connect us to one another.

What is your story? What life-altering event have you experienced that has put you on your journey in life? I believe the two platforms in this world where stories have the biggest potential to transform the lives of those who hear the message is the stage and a book. You are about to read the powerful stories of 24 entrepreneurs in this book. Many of these authors also share their messages speaking from the stage. They know their core genius, and they are extremely engaging.

Any entrepreneur who knows their core genius and creates a strategically designed talk or writes a book around their core genius will be magnetic and memorable. Do you know your core genius? If you know your core genius and you build your business core profits around your core genius, you can speak your way, and write your way to over 100K! When I say speak your way or write your way to over 100K, I mean that you can do that in just one talk and in just one book!

Identifying your core genius is absolutely the most important critical first step to designing a signature talk or writing a book that will highlight your expertise, attract your ideal clients, and turn your business into a revenue-generating machine.

Let's break down the words core genius. When you think of the word core, what comes to mind? I think about what God created me to do. What did God create you to do? What do you think about when you think of the word genius? I think your genius is what you've become an expert in and what you have studied. Therefore, if you combine what you were created for — your core — along with the expert study that you've done — your genius — that becomes your core genius!

It's challenging to identify your core genius for yourself. The reason it is challenging is that it's such an intricate part of who you are. In fact, the work you do in your core genius comes so easy for you that you don't even think it's that special. It's just how you are. It's how you think. It's your own unique perspective. It's what you do measurably better than others. It's what makes you so special.

Your core genius needs to be at the center of your branding, your messaging, your core business profit centers, and especially your signature talk and your book.

I believe that assisting entrepreneurs to identify their core genius is my core genius! When I do this with my clients, I usually get three reactions:

1. They start to cry because they finally feel they have a way to really explain what they do and what makes them special and unique.

2. They start to laugh because they get very excited about their confusion going away, and they can see clearly how to apply all the various strategies they are pursuing and learning to their business.

3. They look me in the eyes and calmly and confidently say YES! YES! YES! as their heads nod up and down, with a look in their eyes of total peace and a knowing look that they now have discovered the missing piece that they needed to soar in their business.

You now know the core genius foundation that is needed to speak your way or write your way to over 100K!

I invite you to dive into these powerful "Voices of Truth" stories. Each story highlights the author's core genius. Be prepared to be inspired, to be emotionally moved, to learn a lesson, and to become connected with these amazing authors. Be sure to take advantage of the author's valuable gifts offered at the end of each of their stories.

Jen Coffel

CEO of Engaging Speakers

"Jen Coffel is the type of person who always gives more than she receives, and if you have the opportunity to know her or work with her, I cannot recommend her enough."

—Jack Canfield
Coauthor of the *Chicken Soup for the Soul*® series
and *The Success Principles*™

Table of Contents

Gail Brown

You Have a Message the World Needs to Hear

"The two most important days of your life are the day you were born and the day you find out why."

—Mark Twain

I truly believe that God has given each of us a message that is uniquely ours. Our responsibility is to make a positive impact on the world with the message we've been given. The world needs hope and inspiration more than ever. Lives can be changed for the better... if you have the courage to deliver your message.

Courage was something I personally needed to build, when it came to sharing my message. Being an introvert, I was apprehensive about putting myself in situations where I didn't feel safe. After I experienced a powerful health transformation, I knew that sharing my story could help many people take charge of their health. I knew I had to find a safe place to learn the skills I needed to share my message in an effective way to grow my business.

I understood that networking had to become part of my life. By learning to network, I became more comfortable building relationships with others. As a result, my health and wellness business began to grow. I learned to use the tips and strategies I'd learned from my time of being a trainer in several industries to inspire my audience to connect with me and take charge of their health. The more I shared my story, the more clients, and referrals I received. These changes allowed my business to grow.

I discovered that several other networking friends were also using public speaking as a way to successfully market and grow their businesses. One day in 2003, I thought, *"What if all of my networking friends who were sharing their stories and I could get together regularly to share ideas on how to improve and build our speaking skills, share speaking opportunities and resources, and support each other in business and in life?"*

I shared my idea with my friend, Tom Gosche. At the time, Tom was the Regional Area Director for BNI. Tom loved the idea and said, "Let's do it!" Therefore, in March 2003, Engaging Speakers was born.

Over the last 19 years, Engaging Speakers has grown nationally. It has helped hundreds of business owners, entrepreneurs, non-profit professionals, speakers, and authors speak their way to more business. I like to say that at Engaging Speakers, we help you define your message, refine it, and find the audience that is best served by your message.

So, where do you begin? Let's start by…

Defining Your Message

1. A message is a communication transmitted via a messenger. That's you! You will deliver that message because of the unique life experiences that have equipped you to do so. Your *Mess* becomes your *Message*. Most times, your message comes as a result of the difficulties you have lived through; and you have learned something that can help someone else live their best life. All the tears, the anxiety, and the heartbreaking things, as well as the joyful things that happen to us, can **tell a story**. That story can impact and change lives.

2. Get clear on what your singular, overarching message is. Do a brain dump or mind-map to get things on paper (or on a computer screen), so you can visually see what lessons you have learned from the *Messes* in your life. You can also see how those lessons can benefit others.

3. One way to structure your key message at the core of your message

map is to use an "XYZ" statement. Fill in the blanks: "I do X, for Y, so they can Z." Example: "Engaging Speakers provides a safe, supportive community for business owners, entrepreneurs, professionals, speakers, and authors to learn to define their message, refine it, and find the audience best served by their message, so they can grow their business and make an impact on the world."

Refining Your Message

1. Once you have defined your message, it is important to refine it. It's time to drill down to what is unique about your message; specifically, how it can help others. List what problems your message can solve for them and how it will improve their lives as a result.

2. Zero in on who you want to serve. Your message may serve many populations. However, it's important to refine to only the one or two groups you will focus on in the beginning.

3. Identify several ways you can serve audiences based on their learning styles or preferences: presentations, retreats, workshops, seminars, articles, blogs, books, webinars, online courses, etc.

Find the Audience That is Best Served by Your Message

1. Now that you know your ideal audience, it is time to find them. Knowing who your audience is will give you clues as to where they are. Study who they are (age, general habits, and behaviors, income levels, etc.) and develop your audience avatar.

2. Where do they hang out? Are they millennials who are online a lot? Are they burned-out business owners looking for a lifeline? Are they frazzled moms who need to know that someone understands? Is it someone who has lost hope and needs a reason to keep going? Find them. Right now, someone is praying for your message.

3. Put your message where your audience is. It could be in person, in print, or online. Be there for them, just as someone was there for you.

If going at it alone feels overwhelming, I encourage you to consider checking out Engaging Speakers, www.EngagingSpeakers.com. Engaging Speakers is a safe, supportive community ready to support you and help you speak your way to more business.

It has been one of the greatest joys of my life to see our Engaging Speakers members courageously take their unique message out to a waiting, wounded world and find the purpose and the passion that was planted in their hearts, and become life-changers. Your message changes YOU, as it changes others!

I would love to accompany you on your journey to sharing your message with the world. I have a very special gift for you… a copy of my "10 Secrets to Becoming an Inspiring Speaker." Please reach out to me and let me know how we can serve you.

Gail Brown

As Founder of Engaging Speakers, Gail Brown believes that everyone has a powerful message to share with the world. For each message, there is someone who needs that message to live his or her best life.

Bringing 40+ years of experience as a top trainer and entrepreneur in the hospitality and network marketing industries, Gail consistently charms audiences by meeting them where they are, with humor and compassion.

Her combination of passion and business acumen uniquely suits her to teach how any business owner can establish themselves as the expert in their field through public speaking, communicating a heart-centered message that gets results.

An experienced yet introverted speaker, Gail created the community she herself sought when she co-founded Engaging Speakers in 2003: a collaborative, non-competitive network of speakers, mentors, and resources.

Engaging Speakers is a safe space for speakers to develop, grow and practice, speaking their way to more business and propelling their valuable message into the world.

Personally mentored by Mary Kay Ash, the founder of Mary Kay Cosmetics, Gail still lives by the words Mary Kay shared in her Dallas home: "Always put God first, your family second, and your career third, and you will be a success in business and in life."

One of her most treasured words of praise are from a Managing Director for eWomen Network: "Gail is a dynamic leader, whose integrity and enthusiasm are only surpassed by her passion to help others achieve their personal best."

Gail's focus has always been on helping others benefit from her journey and cultivating relationships in an environment where people know that they belong and that what they have to say is important.

Gail Brown
Engaging Speakers
Winnebago, IL
630-689-7405
Gail@EngagingSpeakers.com
www.EngagingSpeakers.com

---

10 Secrets to Becoming an Inspiring Speaker

10 Secrets to Becoming an Inspiring Speaker will assist you in learning what secrets you'll need to build an emotional connection with your audience and inspire them to change their lives. Your goal is to inspire your audience to move forward toward their goals.

10SecretsToBecomingAnInspiringSpeaker.com

Dr. Miriam Divinsky

Conscious Living:
How to Become Who You Are Meant to Be

"The Game of Success is not one game. It is TWO."

—Bruce Dickson

"The reality is that pendulum and other dowsing tools are excellent methods for communicating with the Voice of God."

—Susan Shumsky, D.D.

Ask yourself: Are you living the life you came here to live? Are you living your highest gift? Are you living your full potential?

Albert Einstein told us: *"Everyone is a genius. But if you judge a fish on its ability to climb a tree, it will live its whole life believing it is stupid."*

Who are you? How can you get to the state of consciousness that allows you to live the life you choose, have the success you desire and deserve, and live your best life?

What if I tell you that you are a spiritual being having a human experience? That you are a multidimensional being and your Higher Self is your Christ Self, and I AM Presence (Elizabeth Claire Prophet).

What if I tell you that your Outer Game of Success (your success in your life and your business) is a function of your Inner Game, the level of vibrational alignment with your Higher Self?

Your level of success is a reflection of congruency between your Outer

Game and your Inner Game. That is defined by alignment with who you really are, your Higher Self.

To say it another way: your Outer Game of business problems are reflections of Inner Game issues: negative emotions, fears, values, and beliefs that are not adequate for you anymore, crises that you did not resolve. As a result, your Dominant vibration is not congruent with your Higher Self vibration. How can we "upgrade" our Inner Game? How can we facilitate the state of consciousness that is aligned with Higher Self vibration?

We Will Address Two Aspects of This Process:

- The Spiritual Laws that enable us to master conscious living.

- The way to make our whole consciousness (all part of it, conscious, subconscious, and unconscious) align with our higher consciousness by Dowsing.

Let's start with Spiritual Laws that we need to live by to achieve this higher consciousness, to upgrade our Inner Game.

The prerequisite to deep understanding Spiritual Laws, is to understand the principle: AS WITHIN SO WITHOUT.

AS WITHIN SO WITHOUT

"Until you can understand that nothing can happen to you, Nothing can ever come to you or be kept from you, Except in accord with your state of consciousness. You do not have the key to life."

—Paul Twitchell

The Universe arranges itself to manifest the reality that reflects our values, beliefs, and attitudes, literally, as within so without. The self-critical person will attract people who reflect that self-criticism, by constantly judging others. The happy person with a high self-acceptance and self-love will attract secure, happy, and loving people into their lives.

The law is really exact: The Universe rearranges itself to bring you what you are according to your dominant vibration. Let's talk about some of the laws.

Law of Attention

This law explains to us how life manifests itself for us. Whatever we give our attention to manifests in our lives to the exact proportion that we give our attention to it. It can be big or small, good or bad, success or failure. Lives are different, according to the expectations of each person. We create our own reality, according to our dominant vibration and our attention to the desired result.

Here is a simple example: Let's imagine that two people would like to manifest a million dollars.

Person #1: He focuses most of his attention on how good it will feel to have that abundance and, therefore, his dominant vibration — and the actions he takes to achieve his goal — are congruent.

Person #2: He is trying to put his attention on having the money, but his dominant vibration reflects his belief that money is very hard to get.

Who do you think has a higher probability of achieving his goal?

The problem is that we often have mixed feelings about what we want. Together with desire for money, we have prejudices and fears about money. Together with desire for a partner, we fear having a broken heart, and we have limited beliefs about our worthiness. Please realize that positive has more power than negative. Focus on positive, and it will have a higher probability to come true. Focus on what you want, and you will attract it to your life.

Law of Flow

We live in a universe comprised of energy, which flows like a river. The Law of Flow governs every area of life. If we hoard money, clothing, ideas, resentments or any negative emotions, there is no space for NEW to come into our life. To allow NEW into our life, we must let go of the old, repressed emotions, fears, and limiting beliefs.

"Nature does not allow vacuum, so something always moves into an empty space. Your task is to ensure it is something better."

—Diane Cooper

As soon as we release beliefs and emotions that do not serve our goal, we open ourselves for NEW to come in. We can use the Law of Flow to facilitate a connection with who we are meant to be. Abundance and Prosperity result, when we balance outflow with the inflow.

"Go with the flow and you will reach the Source."

—Diane Cooper

Law of Abundance

"Abundance means flowing the love, joy, happiness, prosperity, success, vitality, laughter, generosity, and all the good in life."

—Diane Cooper

Our life is abundant when we live with the higher qualities of life. Abundance is our birthright. Then what stops us from living in abundance?

The level of consciousness, thoughts, beliefs, how we perceive our deservability, our level of self-love, self-esteem, and self-acceptance can create barriers to receiving what we want because they do not reflect who we are.

The Law of Abundance works consistently: if you want more friends, be friendly to others. If you want more happiness, remember that your beliefs and memories can be released and replaced with better ones by Dowsing. All good things of life and material things flow to us when we have a consciousness of abundance.

Law of Clarity of Intention

"The moment you make a clear decision, a light goes over your head. The Powers that be in the universe sees this light and aligns behind you to manifest your vision."

"Clarity opens the doors to your future. Speak clearly to the Universe about your wants and needs. Clear thoughts and intentions draw from the Universe that which you require for your life. Never forget you are the Master. It is your right to order what you need and to expect your order to be fulfilled."

—Diane Cooper

Clarity is the first step to freedom and the achievement of your heart's desire. When your intentions are noble and honorable, you will be rewarded for the purity of your ideas. An intention is like an arrow in flight. Nothing can deflect it, so aim carefully.

Law of Prosperity

The Spiritual Laws that cause you to flourish or to wither are the same. They respond to your dominant vibration. Limiting beliefs, fears, and unresolved negative emotions lower your dominant vibration.

When we replace all of them with positive beliefs and emotions, raising our baselines of deservability, self-esteem, self-acceptance, self-love, inner peace, and joy, our dominant vibration is high and Spiritual Laws respond to it.

The Universe responds to our consciousness. If a person belonged to a religious order and took a vow of poverty in his or her past life, and this vow is still active in the person's consciousness, the person will feel guilty about money. We can release all non-beneficial vows with Dowsing, and we can experience a change of vibration and, consequently, change our relationship with money.

The most spiritual attitude is to have money and use it wisely. It is not spiritual to worry about money. In fact, it is quite unproductive. To worry about money is like praying for not having it. Why? Because worry is attention with fear. It lowers our dominant vibration and attracts the absence of money.

Prosperity means having a sense of financial well-being. Prosperity is an acceptance of our abundance birthright and the responsibility and power that comes with it.

Law of Success

Our beliefs create energy that vibrates around us as a substantial part of our dominant vibration. Success is facilitated with acceptance and believing in oneself. When we release with Dowsing limiting beliefs and replace them with self-acceptance, self-worth, and deservability, we are paving our road to success. Then we are able to do our best and achieve the highest and best for all concerned. Success takes place when our vibration resonates with the vibration of the outcome we desire.

Success is the result when our conscious mind (the place of desired outcome) is congruent with the unconscious mind (the place of our belief system). Success is not a particular achievement — it is a function of our state of mind, congruent with our Higher Self.

We've just discussed the Spiritual Laws that impact and govern our state of consciousness, our Inner Game. Living according to these Spiritual Laws allows us to take an important step in living our true potential and our highest gift. Our unconscious and conscious minds need to be congruent for achieving our true potential. Do you live your highest gift? Do you live your true potential?

As I mentioned above, the technology that allows us to reveal our true gift and to release all blocks to living that gift is Dowsing. We do not become Spirit when we move on to the Spirit World when we die. We are Spirit NOW. The physical "you" houses your consciousness. That consciousness is the real you. That consciousness that is in every living thing is Omnipresent.

Quantum Physics has proven that everything exists in a field of all possibilities until observed by consciousness. This means consciousness is creative. It is a source of all awareness. It is all-knowing. Every person is a focus of One Mind. We can intentionally access this state of consciousness with Dowsing, transcend the limitations of ordinary awareness, and be open to a higher level of mastery and wisdom.

Now, Let Us Summarize What We Have Just Discussed

You always act within the Universal Mind. However, what kind of results your action will bring you depends on how you act within the infinite power of the Universal Mind, on what level you are living the fundamental spiritual laws.

Let's talk for a moment about why Dowsing allows us to become who we were meant to be and live the life of our full potential by upgrading our Inner Game. What is the main problem that Dowsing allows us to resolve?

We understand that The Laws of Abundance and Prosperity work by default or by intent. It is like the gravity law — whether we know about it or not, it is constantly at work. If you live what you want, it is by intent. If you live what you don't want, it is by default.

These Laws deliver into our lives experiences that exactly correspond to our dominant vibration. What constitutes our dominant vibration? Whether we are aware of them or not, our values, beliefs, thoughts, and feelings create our dominant vibration, and consequently, our life experiences. Again, Outer Game is a function of our Inner Game.

With Dowsing we can find, release, and transform all non-beneficial beliefs, values, fears, thoughts, and feelings and bring our unconscious into congruence with our consciousness. This congruence allows us to create by intent rather than by default.

Let us consider the iceberg model of the mind. The tip of the iceberg (what is above the water) represents our conscious mind. That which lies below the water's surface — at least ten times larger than the tip — represents our unconscious mind. The closest part to the water is our subconscious, and the deepest part is our personal superconscious. The vast ocean which connects and supports all icebergs (and everything else in creation) represents One Mind, Universal Field of Energy.

Dowsing allows the conscious mind of the dowser to connect with the clients' unconscious mind and release fears, repressed emotions, traumatic experiences, non-beneficial irrational beliefs — all aspects of the client's unconscious that prevent manifestation by intent. After all that non-beneficial content is released, the dowser works on transforming this energy into beneficial energy.

Finally, the goal of this work is to have the client's unconscious mind be congruent with conscious mind, allowing the person to live by intent, to have what they want and deserve in their lives. This resolves the problem of the client living by default and transforms it into living by intent.

It is interesting to note that quantum physicists now define the reality that mystics have described for thousands of years: the Universe is a Field of Energy. We dowse in that Field. The evolution of science moved our perception of reality from Newtonian physics to Einstein's acknowledgment that perception of reality depends on the viewer's position. According to Quantum Physics: observations change the particles' behavior.

With Dowsing, we can initiate change in the client's reality, by observing and transforming by intent. Dowsing allows the non-local transfer of energy operating at a quantum level. That is very beneficial: it allows the dowser to help to create the client's reality by intent, whether the client is in front of a dowser or halfway around the globe — with the same incredible results.

Let us look together at an example of attitudes of abundance and the blocks for the abundance that can be dowsed out of our conscious and unconscious minds. When your attitude and beliefs about abundance are congruent with your Higher Self beliefs and attitudes, you can manifest by intent.

Let us consider an example of negative beliefs in our unconscious mind that prevent our living by intent that Dowsing can release.

- I am not good enough to deserve abundance.
- Life is a struggle.
- People may take advantage of me.

- I cannot trust anybody.

- Money does not grow on trees.

- It takes money to make money.

- Money is the root of all evil.

- If I have more, someone else will have less.

These negative beliefs can be released and transformed into positive beliefs and attitudes toward abundance.

- I live my full potential.

- I create my life.

- My intention is to create abundant life.

- I believe money is the freedom to live the life I deserve.

- I am creating abundant life by doing what I love.

- I add value to people's lives.

- I am grateful for the money I have.

- Great opportunities come to my attention, and I accept them.

- My ability to earn money is getting better and better.

Now we can really understand why Carl Jung wrote: *"Until you make the unconscious conscious, it will direct your life, and you will call it fate."*

"The privilege of a lifetime is to become who you truly are."

Who are you truly?

You are the Spiritual Being having a human form and an experience of life on Earth. Your purpose is awakening that will be expressed as congruency of your dominant vibration with your Higher Self.

At that time, your Outer Game (your business, your personal life) and your Inner Game (who you truly are) are aligned, your living by intent, fulfilling your true potential and your destiny: a Cocreator with One Mind.

Dr. Miriam Divinsky

Miriam Divinsky, Ph.D., is a business and personal coach, who helps her clients to create their business, professional and personal lives by intent, to live their highest gifts, and fulfill their full potential.

She helps her clients to synchronize their business, "Outer Game of Success," with their "Inner Game of Success," with who they really are.

The synchronization of these two games of life allows her clients to live their professional lives with success and fulfillment and their personal lives with fulfillment and joy.

Miriam Divinsky has been featured in "Who's Who National Registry" and "Who's Who in American Women." She is a Diplomat and Fellow of the Clinical Hypnotherapy Board and listed in "America's Best Therapists."

Dr. Miriam Divinsky
St. Petersburg, FL
978-675-5653
DivinskyMiriam@gmail.com
www.LivingByIntent.com

Dowsing: the Search for Truth

To learn more about how Dowsing can eliminate blocks to the fulfillment of your major desires: financial success, finding a partner, finding your soul purpose, or any other desire you may hold dear to your heart, contact Miriam Divinsky to inquire about attending a future workshop.

Contact Miriam Divinsky at: DivinskyMiriam@gmail.com

Jennifer L. Jost
Diamond Ring Dream

All I wanted was to be loved, adored, and cherished. At the age of 19, the day had arrived. I had my diamond ring. My life was set. The prince rescued me. At least, that is what I thought.

Three Shots Were Fired

The last 24 hours had been a nightmare…

My husband had broken the court order and had my kids again. He had somehow tracked me down and began verbally threatening me and brandishing a gun. I was terrified, so I went to the police for help. Since we had no idea where he went or how to find him, they said there was nothing they could do. It sounds crazy, but for some reason, I drove to the gas station and bought a pack of cigarettes. I didn't smoke, never have, but I thought it would help me calm down. I went to a friend's house for support, and all I could do was pace, for hours. It was one of the longest nights of my life. I was completely terrified! All I could do was breathe and get through it, moment by moment.

The long minutes, turned to scary hours. I had to go to work. I had no idea what the day would bring, but I had to go through the motions. Since he knew what time I had to be at work, he was waiting for me to arrive. He pulled up in a rented van with my 5-year-old daughter on his lap with a gun to her head. He said, "Get in the car, now!"

Terrified, adrenaline-rushing, I became a mother bear immediately. I jumped in the van, grabbed my daughter, and put her on my lap. I hugged her and said, "Dad's just being silly. Don't even worry." My heart was racing. I looked in the backseat and saw that my 8-year-old son was lying down, but he was okay. I reached back and held his hand, trying to express that everything would be okay. At the same time, there were many horrible scenarios racing through my head. I knew he would hurt me but never the kids.

We arrived at my house. At gunpoint, he demanded that I go inside the house, leaving the kids in the van. He threw me a duffel bag full of rope and duct tape and yelled: "Put the rope on, tie your hands up." After an hour, the phone started ringing off the hook. My employees were calling. I had to go to work. He said that I could go to work. He and the kids would follow me. They sat outside for almost an hour. As soon as they left, I ran across the street to the payphone.

The Nightmare Begins

That 911 call started the 11-hour hostage negotiation. It was the worst day of my life.

I was at a neighbor's house, watching the police negotiating with my husband, who was holding my children hostage in our master bedroom.

After 11 hours, a 10-minute ultimatum was given to him to come out, or they would storm in. Three shots were fired. He took the lives of my children, Nicholas and Cheri', and himself in my master closet, when I was 29 years old.

Big breath here…

And again…

Now breathe again with me…

How did I get here? I never could have imagined this day.

The American Dream

I thought my life was great. On the outside, my family looked amazing (fake truth). I bought my parents' business three years into the marriage. We had two businesses along with rental properties. We made good money, had a beautiful huge house, a maroon Jaguar, LeBaron convertible, and a brand new custom blue step-side Chevy truck. You know, it was The American Dream. On the outside, we looked great. On the inside, I just could not breathe.

Have you ever woken up and felt that heavyweight sitting on your chest?

I was very unhappy and scared to death at the same time. I had no idea who I was. It had been ten years of emotional abuse that happened gradually. I did not realize that I was completely losing myself, my truth, and my power.

I started attending church. I started going to therapy. I met new friends and was in search mode. I needed to DO something. Find my voice.

I ended up asking him for a divorce. It did not go well. It was six months of hell. I don't know if you've ever seen someone flip a switch to scary rage. It was like you had just literally seen a transformation into a completely different person. He wanted to try couples therapy. I just wanted a safe place to get out of the marriage. I moved into the spare bedroom, which helped a bit. I drew a boundary. There would be no more sex! He used to walk around my bed with a gun down to his side, silent but powerful. I got the message. Divorce equals death.

I don't even think I told my therapist about that nightly ritual because, my fake belief, I should be perfect. I should be able to handle anything. He finally moved out of the house. Through the court process, he had supervised visitation rights with his family member as the supervisor.

My Choice to Live

How am I still here, and why am I still here? I had to find a reason to get out of bed in the morning. I tried therapy three times a week, cried uncontrollably, and stayed away from the outside world. It was then recommended that I go to a grief group for parents who had also lost children. This group saved my life. When I saw people getting on with life after losing a child, I knew I could. I remember a couple that sobbed every week, just sobbed and sobbed every single week. There was also a woman that handled grief with such grace. When I found out that the couple had lost their son five years earlier, I said to myself,

"There's no way that I can continue living with this level of excruciating pain for years." So……..

I made a CHOICE to get through the grief process and to live and find my voice. I made a choice to live on purpose and find my purpose. I had no idea what my purpose was at that point. I just knew I lived for a reason. I had to make a difference with my life and honor my children. I now know without a doubt, that I am here on this planet to help empower people.

We all have a choice. What choice are you making with your life?

After I thought my life was over and I made my choice to live, I had to determine my next actions. I felt inside, I was a mom and would always be a mom. I married my boyfriend, who I was dating at the time. He showed up for me at the hospital, when I had to see my children, Nicholas and Cheri' and they were pronounced dead. I was a mess. We were married two years later. My daughter Journey was born one year later, and my son Parker, thirteen months after that. We lived happily ever after. NOT, we were divorced several years later. I remarried an amazing firefighter. I now have three amazing adult stepchildren. It was my blessing to support them growing up. We were also divorced, and he is happily remarried. You see, I did not think that I was worthy of love, until I excavated my hidden beliefs with my coach and supportive tribe. I now have an abundance of love and joy every day. It is no wonder that I became a Certified Divorce Financial Analyst. I know this process well. Maybe the fourth time will be the charm. I believe we all just want and deserve to be loved, adored, and cherished.

Three Steps to Survive Trauma

I will share my first three steps of how I survived the most unimaginable experience. I hope it helps you to realize that you can get through anything and even find amazing love and joy inside. Then learn to let love in.

Step 1

Make a Choice

Once we make a choice, our brain can relax. As a result, creativity can flow and focus on the future, not the past. Who knows what you can create, once a choice is made? By making a choice, it allowed me to create my businesses. I am honoring my grief experience and my love for Nicholas and Cheri' every day. Their birthstone is Diamond, since they were both born in April. My business is Diamond Life Planning. Just think about what you can create. I would have never thought I would be called the money woman. Go figure.

This is where I use the F WORD. Traditionally, we used the pros and cons of making a choice. The modern way is to elicit your Emotions and Feelings. When making a choice, FEEL how it would be with each of the outcomes. I promise that it will give you a more aligned answer to your purpose and your truth. Even if you do not know your purpose just yet, FEEL your way to your CHOICE.

According to a UNC-TV report, Americans make 35,000 conscious choices a day. This takes brainpower. Once we make a choice, we have much more space to receive love and amazing experiences, instead of spending time and energy making a choice.

My Choice: I choose to live. I choose to live a life of joy, love, and abundance. I choose to live a life of service and make a difference.

Step 2

Know Your Why

Now that you've made the choice, you are on your way to YOUR WHY. What is your Why? Why do you get up in the morning? Why do you abide by societal rules? Knowing your why is not enough. I am asking you to uplevel your experience. Share your why. Share it with people you trust and who care deeply about your well-being. People need to earn our trust and earn our truth.

We need to feel safe, not judged. When you feel safe, share your WHY. It makes you authentic. It makes you real. You might even change your why. It could look different after the year's pass.

Your Why is important because when life happens (shit hits the fan), you have your WHY to grab onto. At times, it can be your lifeboat. Knowing and sharing your why will bring people in your life to support your WHY. Shout it to the universe! I am here, and this is WHY!

My Why: I wake up every morning knowing that I am here to empower people to live their lives in joy, love, and abundance. As Oprah would say, "Live their best life."

Step 3

Share Your Story

We all have a story or many, many stories. It could be a small event or a trauma you have faced and overcome. Positive stories are amazing, such as the National Advisor of the Year Award, which I won. That was so amazing. My daughter, Journey, was there watching me walk across the stage and receive my award. Very few women have received it. I was a rock star that week. Women stopped me throughout the day and wanted to find out how I accomplished such an award. It was my first experience in mentoring.

Most of us hate to brag, so we hold back on sharing our positive stories. I ask that you share your story. Share both positive and scary stories. As Brene Brown states in her book, *Daring Greatly*, "It takes courage to be vulnerable." Secrets create shame, so sharing our vulnerabilities releases trapped negative emotions in our bodies. The 12-step programs have this point down well. When I was completely lost after my children passed, I could only gain a glimpse of what moving on could look like from other parents who had lost children. The more we share our stories, the more we find our tribes. The more we see, the more we are alike than different. As Oprah says, "People just want to be seen and heard." Find your safe people and share. A thought is eternal, until it is unthought or rethought.

According to Heathline.com, "When toxic shame lingers without resolution, the desire to hide from it or escape from yourself can lead to potentially harmful behavior, like substance misuse or self-harm." Since I work with people and money, you would be surprised how much this shame shows up in your relationship with money. Feeling worthy also leads to feeling worthy of abundance and love as well. This could be your number one tip for your finances. Honoring my vulnerabilities and loving myself as I am, I can truthfully say I am perfectly imperfect and proud of it. I recommend asking for help. I have had many amazing coaches and mentors that have helped me through my past. Don't go it alone. Share your story.

My Story: Well, it is in print now, wow. I also am a speaker sharing my story, sharing my truth. As imperfect as it is, it is real and mine.

In summary:

1. Make a Choice

2. Know Your Why

3. Share Your Story

We walk in our path and find our purpose and our truth. Continuing these steps allow us to show up every day in our purpose and lead our purposeful life. I'm living my purpose every day. I help empower people. I choose to do that around money. We all deserve to love our lifestyle in joy, love, and abundance.

"We cannot love anything or anyone, without loving ourselves first."

—Lucille Ball

I will now finish up, as I do every client with homework. Here is your optional list, of course. Good luck:

1. Make a list of all your wonderful attributes. What have you accomplished? What's great about you? If you have trouble with making this simple list, it is your focus now.

My example: I am smart. I am honest. I am empathetic. I am an amazing speaker.

2. Celebrate your wins, no matter how small you think they are. The big ones are easy. My clients create their money Dance. It is important to feel joy and celebration in our whole body. It shouldn't be just empty words or thoughts. Get up and shake your body and sing or shout! Celebrate now and often. Make it a family tradition.

My example: Finishing this chapter, talk about being vulnerable. You bet I am dancing!

3. Write down 100 things that you love. Have fun with this one. Feel the feelings when you write them down. Some of my clients have trouble with this list. Look at this list every day until it is easy to add more.

My example: Hot shower, purple, rock n roll, my pillow, and my car.

I appreciate your time spent reading this book. We are all unique diamonds. Shine in your life! If I have touched you and you would like to connect, message me at www.JenniferJost.com.

Sending you Joy, Love, and Abundance!

Jennifer L. Jost

Jennifer L. Jost, Certified Divorce Analyst (CDFA)®, Certified Money Coach (CMC)®, and is an award-winning Speaker and Wealth Advisor. As National Associate Advisor of the Year, Presidents Club, and Inner Circle, she qualified for the Million Dollar Round Table. She gives back by being a Certified Grief Counselor and philanthropist helping women and girls worldwide. With the highest level of commitment as a fiduciary, Jennifer cares for her clients as a Registered Investment Advisor.

With over 30 years of experience as a successful business owner and meeting with thousands of people as their trusted Wealth Advisor and Money Coach, she addresses much more than the rate of return. Jennifer believes our emotions around money are not being addressed in the traditional financial services industry. Through her proven success system, she takes her clients through all the stages of wealth to gain the 3C's — Clarity, Confidence, and Control. This leads them to financial freedom.

However, it's through her own personal story of trials to triumph where Jennifer's real magic and power lies. On her journey from grief to reclaiming life, she found meaning in serving others and guiding women on their path to empowerment. As Jennifer says, "Women feeling worthy of wealth will change this world!" She knows she is here for a reason and lives daily in her joy!

Jennifer L. Jost
Diamond Life Planning
JJ@DiamondLifeWealth.com
www.JenniferJost.com
www.DiamondLifePlanning.com

Financial Freedom Starts with Your Money Mindset

Discover FINANCIAL FREEDOM… start living your desired life.

You Will Receive Access to My Three Amazing Videos:

1. Three Barriers To Wealth

2. Master Your Money Mindset

3. Money Success System

www.JennifersGift.com

Judy Hahn

Funky to Fabulous

It was only seven a.m. that March 2020 morning when I walked into the kitchen and was bombarded by the latest news. It was all about this worldwide pandemic, and I knew it would send me into a downward spiral, so I decided it was the perfect time to escape, even if just for a quick trip to the grocery store. I grabbed my purse and headed for the car.

Still trying to shake off what I had heard, I managed to smile to myself as I passed the gas station on the corner. Years ago, I routinely stopped there for my sugar fixes. It was either that or Panera, where stopping for a chocolate chip cookie had become three cookies... and then six.

Yes, there were a few "have to have" ice cream days over the last 18 months. However, as a proud "recovering" sugar addict, I felt great that I had conquered my former emotional eating/cravings and "have to have" turned into not having at all. Those cravings surely would have reared their ugly heads during a very unpredictable and highly stressful worldwide health crisis, such as COVID-19. To top it off, I also endured the stress and anxiety of client cancellations (as so many business owners experienced during 2020). But even still, I managed to remain sugar-free!

You see, I had made a commitment to myself to age gracefully, without the chronic health issues that so many people my age experience, and everything seemed to be going according to plan. Or so I thought. During an annual physical, my bloodwork showed otherwise. If this bloodwork had belonged to one of my clients, we would be having a conversation about insulin resistance, what it means and why it's important to begin working on reversing it. This is because insulin resistance can lead to diabetes, if ignored. However, it wasn't a client's bloodwork. It was mine. To say that I was shocked and surprised would be an understatement.

I knew that before COVID, my activity level was okay but needed some improvement. I wasn't obese (but could lose a few pounds for vanity's sake). My blood pressure was perfect. I also ate very little red meat. My diet consisted of lots of organic veggies, organic chicken and different wild fishes, and gluten-free grains. I was eating healthy. So what happened?

What's Wrong with the Energizer Bunny?

Although not on my shopping list, bags and bags of organic, Skinny Popcorn made their way regularly to our house. Somehow, it never registered on my recovering sugar addict's radar. After all, I wasn't eating candy, brownies, or chocolate chip cookies. However, now when I stop and think about it, corn is primarily a carbohydrate. To be completely transparent, moderation wasn't the word for my consumption of the popcorn.

But that was just a small part of the problem. In addition to eating way too much popcorn, I was completely ignoring that I was experiencing much more stress than ever before. I know that stress causes cortisol levels to rise, can add belly fat, and can be responsible for the cravings I was experiencing. However, because I didn't have kids to homeschool, a nine-to-five job in a business outside my home, or elderly parents to care for, I wasn't thinking I had the same stress that the rest of the world was experiencing. Although I wasn't watching the news during the pandemic, I was seeing almost nothing but negativity on social media. What I saw there was even worse than watching the news because I was reading awful stories from people who were friends or acquaintances, which made it even more emotionally debilitating and stressful.

Then came the huge energy slumps. There were days when I would be sitting at my computer around 2:30 in the afternoon when I literally couldn't keep my eyes open. It was as if I had hit a wall. I would fold my arms onto my desk and rest my head, dozing at times. It was not for long, but exhaustion would come over me. I couldn't continue working. It sounded like what some of my clients explained to me happened to them in the afternoons. This type of energy slump was very out of the norm for me. I am usually so full of energy that close friends call me "the energizer bunny."

I was in denial, thinking it was due to a bad night's sleep, instead of realizing this was part of what was going on inside my body. I wasn't connecting that in my attempts to push through and finish my work, I ate so I wouldn't need to take those little naps. I needed an energy boost because my blood sugar was crashing, so I reached for a huge bowl of Skinny Popcorn or a whole box of gluten-free crackers. No moderation here. From my body's standpoint, none of that was different from a candy bar.

In addition to being tired mid-day, I was also definitely more unfocused. I called it the "bright, shiny, object" syndrome. However, it was different. It felt more like what my clients call "brain fog." It was definitely affecting my productivity.

My productivity wasn't the only thing that was impacted. So was my mood. On one of those "have to have" ice cream days, I got very emotional. I was crying, being super negative, and beating myself up unmercifully. I called my best friend since I was out of control and needed her to talk me down. During the conversation, she asked me if I happened to have eaten a large quantity of candy or ice cream. At first, I was upset with her for getting off the subject. However, I then had a huge "aha," recognizing the effects of my old nemesis... sugar — but this emotional upset was from the withdrawal effects of it rather than eating it.

Those old sugar days were now so far behind me that I wasn't seeing it was just the effects of sugar on my body... the moodiness, the irritability, and the depression-like symptoms. It was sugar/carb addict behavior, which was to search out comfort food (for me, that was anything with sugar) when I was frustrated, stressed, and saddened by external things over which I had no control. And, since I wasn't feeding the addiction, it was still as if I was experiencing the same withdrawal symptoms as a drug addict.

The In-Person Dilemma

Fast forward to the world starting to re-open after mandatory shut-downs. We were doing more things in person. People started to have in-person networking events. I was even registered to go to a conference in a few months. I also planned to have a photoshoot at that time. I looked at the clothes in my closet and tried on a few things. With wearing workout clothes for the last year (you know those pants that give at the waist), I didn't have a single thing I could comfortably put on my body. I was so disheartened.

It was at that moment I realized how much weight I had gained and how out of shape I was. I hadn't been able to go to the gym and did nothing but work obsessively from dawn to dark, adding positive value to my private Facebook group by offering laugh yoga classes, grief support, and much more. With that realization came the tears and not wanting to attend the event because I didn't feel confident in myself, even if my business clothes had fit.

The Moment of Truth

While we were re-emerging from lock-downs, I was working with one of my clients, and more than ever, I was resonating with the information she shared with me. She felt very strongly that the reason she wasn't losing weight had to do with menopause. It is important to respect the intuition of my clients because no one knows their body better than they do, including me. Therefore, we began her health journey, by doing hormone testing.

What we found was that an unrecognized chronic high-stress level, food choices, and lifestyle habits were contributing to the issues, along with some hormone issues from menopause. With how much my client's situation resonated with me (and because at times I like to do what I am having my clients do, just to experience it myself), I decided I would ask my doctor to have a few extra tests done. My annual physical was due anyway. Remember the blood work that showed up from earlier? This was it.

The results came. I was now a statistic. I was one out of three people in the U.S. who could be told by their doctor that they had what is called "Prediabetes." I was one of the nine out of ten people who have it but are not at all aware they have it!

I compared my previous blood test and saw an upward trend in the numbers. I knew if I continued my carb intake and high-stress levels, my body would continue to compensate for my choices thanks to its innate brilliance and ability to have organs assist each other to keep it functioning. My education in functional medicine principles had also taught me that the increase in my cholesterol numbers could be related to my body's inability to regulate my blood sugar and insulin, increasing other health risks, like heart disease and fatty liver.

I Need My Own Services

It was time to be my own client, fill out my health history form, my detailed symptom questionnaire, create a "map" of interconnectedness, look at a timeline and write up a report to go along with it. It was time to be in integrity with myself as a functional medicine wellness coach, get down to business, and live my truth. Otherwise, I was an imposter.

I thought about it for a while and realized that my doctor really hadn't indicated that I had any pressing health issues. My cholesterol and triglyceride numbers were on the high side, but nothing I couldn't get under control.

Since I was primarily "fine," I could continue as I had been doing with no concerns about a future that included diabetes. However, I knew if the numbers kept trending upwards, I might eventually end up with a formal diagnosis of diabetes and high cholesterol/triglycerides. There would be a whole new set of issues to resolve and conversations to have. If that happened, it would take a much longer time to reverse the situation than if it had been caught earlier.

However, I realized that there was no great secret in what needed to be done. I had the knowledge I needed to help myself turn this around. If there is one thing I know, this condition and even diabetes are reversible.

My Formula for Change

My formula for any change was a simple one but not necessarily an easy one. It is AWARENESS + ACTION + ACCOUNTABILITY = THE TRANSFORMATION YOU DESIRE. It comes down to these three steps that I'm sharing with you, so your journey can be different.

AWARENESS:

It doesn't really matter how you get there. However, without awareness, there isn't a reason to change. Whether you have symptoms, a yearly checkup, and your doctor isn't happy with your numbers, or you intuitively know something is off, what's important is you're starting to notice something isn't quite right. Something has triggered you to start questioning what is going on in your body. That questioning and wondering is awareness.

ACTION:

Awareness without action leaves you exactly where you started. Having filled out the appropriate paperwork (as I would have any client do) gave me some insight on where to start. It was the same place I started with any client. It is the low-hanging fruit, as we call it. These are the foundational things that need to be in place, no matter what a person is suffering from.

It was about starting with the basics and creating a plan I could stick to, and that made sense for me. I had to take a hard look at how, what, and when I was eating and drinking. This was a look at diet, nutrition, and hydration to start. It was about looking at the pantry to see what was there and determining if I had become lax with what I was buying by checking my labels for hidden sugars. I also had to look at why I was eating and consider how I was dealing with food in my life. It was the emotional aspect. I also needed to look at my sleep. Health is always about balancing body, mind, and spirit.

ACCOUNTABILITY:

How was I going to decide to be my best client and work collaboratively with myself on everything I worked on with my clients? It was about enlisting resources for support if I needed them and about doing the research and deciding what might work the best for me as my own client. The truth is that a client is NOT accountable to someone else. It is the commitment they have to their own health and well-being that truly keeps them accountable to themselves, their goals, and living their best lives.

Health is a Journey, Not a Destination

I haven't done any new bloodwork. However, I already know from all the baby steps I have taken over these last several months that this situation will be all (or mostly) turned around when I do get it done. Just like with my clients, I made recommendations for myself. Then, in my role as my client, I decided if they felt right or if I thought I might like to try a different route.

Treating myself like a client has been about reminding myself it is a process. It is kind of like peeling an onion, where I might encounter something new along the way that I would then also have to address. However, I made a choice. I chose my health because at 69 years old, there is no way I will accept that my plans for the future will be detoured by health issues. Knowing that these were things that I could reverse, there was no excuse not to do so.

I love that I get up and out to move my body first thing in the morning, that I stay hydrated, have great sleep habits, have lots of options for stress management, and cravings are few and far between. I have found a way to eat that seems to agree with me and what my unique body needs for good health. I even started journaling again, which, although not my favorite activity, I was open to trying.

I didn't get unhealthy overnight. The stage was set from a very young age. Therefore, getting healthy isn't going to happen tomorrow. As I continue my health journey, I must remain curious about my health and create the same judgment-free zone for myself that I do for my clients. Like life in general, getting healthy is about making choices and living with the consequences (good or bad).

I am fortunate to have had the knowledge that allowed me to recognize what was truly going on inside my body and to have such a vast toolbox of things to help myself turn my health around. Achieving optimal health is a work in progress. There is no magic pill or shortcut to go from unhealthy to healthy. The body can heal itself. It just needs a little help and time. Once the root cause is addressed, the symptoms begin to subside or go away completely.

This experience was a gift. If I had continued the same path I was on, I could have ended up with a serious health condition in the next 10+ years. In some way, those Panera runs, my former sugar addiction, and becoming my own client have reinforced my passion and commitment to help others live life to its fullest, thriving, not just surviving, and feeling fabulous (not funky).

Judy Hahn

Judy Hahn is a recovering sugar addict, emotional eater, and someone who brought herself back from the brink of a nervous breakdown caused by the stress of her corporate job. Known as the "it's not all in your head health expert," she helps motivated women go from feeling funky to feeling fabulous.

She is a Functional Medicine Wellness Coach. She is the founder and owner of Hahn Holistic Health and is also a Nationally Board-Certified Health and Wellness Coach, a Certified Integrative Nutrition Coach, a Certified International Health Coach, and a Certified Quantum Coach. With over 30 years in a variety of service and client relations positions coupled with her deep curiosity about the human body, Judy is perfect for this very client-centric health model. Judy puzzle-pieces symptoms together to discover the root cause of a client's "dis-ease."

A lifelong learner, she continues her studies at the School of Applied Function Medicine and the Academy of Functional Wellness.

Judy is recognized as an expert and a pioneer in her field. Her articles have been published in Best Holistic Life Magazine, where she continues to write with unbridled joy as she loves to share her passion. She also makes frequent appearances on health and wellness-related podcasts (links can be found on her website www.HahnHolisticHealth.com).

On a personal note, Judy has been married to her husband, Jerry, for 36 years and is the mom to Sophie and Maggie, two adorable soft-coated wheaten terriers. When she isn't working with clients or doing research, you'll find her out in nature — walking, hiking, kayaking, or gardening. Judy is also an avid traveler and loves to speak French or Spanish any chance she gets!

Judy Hahn
Hahn Holistic Health LLC
414-736-8899
Judy@HahnHolisticHealth.com
www.HahnHolisticHealth.com

Functional Medicine... It's All About YOU!

Functional medicine is the medicine of the future. It is focused on prevention, and clients work with their practitioners on nutrition, diet, exercise, stress management, and so much more. The goal is to identify and address the root cause of the disease rather than just address the symptoms someone may be experiencing.

The functional medicine practitioner spends time with his client learning about their history, lifestyle, genetic makeup, the external elements of their lives being the physical and social environment, as well as the internal factors regarding body, mind, and spirit. This patient-centric model of medicine truly looks at each person as a unique individual. The practitioner and client collaborate to achieve the client's health goals.

The four videos will cover:

1. What the heck is Functional Medicine?

2. It's not all in your head.

3. You are not defined by your genes.

4. Optimal health is not complicated.

Scan the QR code to learn how functional medicine can help you.

https://bit.ly/FMed101

Jared N. Silver

From Orthodox Introvert to Competent Presenter

As a young child, adults referred to me as VERY shy. I remember my dad teasing me about my lack of social interaction by comparing me to the Peanuts character, Linus, "I love mankind... it's the PEOPLE I can't stand!"

I had a couple of good friends, but most of the time, I was pretty happy and busy creating, writing, drawing, rebuilding, redesigning, and rewiring "stuff" — bicycles, toys, and household appliances. I was a photo-realistic painter at age eight. I remember winning ribbons at school art shows. I also remember not liking the recognition of being in the spotlight. Being noticed for what I did naturally just didn't make sense.

Ever Feel Like a Freak?

When I was seven years old, my parents were becoming more concerned about socializing their "anti-social kid." They decided that learning to play an instrument might "bring me out of my shell." This was back in the mid-1960s. Classic Rock N' Roll history was being made! The British Invasion was sweeping America. I'm thinking, "Guitar or drums? Hey, this could be fun! Maybe trombone? My 15-year-old brother plays trombone in the school band. Dad played the trombone as a kid."

One week later, we're arriving at the Homewood Music Center. No guitar, no drums, no trombone. Nope. *"Jared, here's your... Accordion!"* A what? Accordion?

Minutes later, two giant adults are strapping a massive instrument onto my little 7-year-old body. They let go — I go down. I am placed into a chair. I hear a quiet voice, *"Mrs. Silver, I'll order a smaller, lighter instrument tomorrow. He will LOVE it!"* Guess what. I never loved it.

As far as the socializing aspect goes, I was not aware of an all-accordion marching band at my school. My accordion recitals were attended by the parents of the other squeezebox pseudo-virtuoso geeks. This childhood story seems funny to me today. However, at that time, it was rather depressing. Had I been able to verbalize my feelings back then, I would have said, *"Mom, Dad, can we please try another approach? I can't seem to blend in with this thing strapped to my body?"* Instead, I made the best of it.

Conducting Business Today Can Feel Like an Accordion Recital

You may be an accomplished presenter or perhaps a professional public speaker. Either way, you've been transacting business in person for years. You can whistle that tune! You KNOW what to say and how to say it. You know how to connect with your audience. Suddenly… everything changed. You now have an accordion strapped to your body, and you ***don't know*** which buttons to push! Technology is — once again — dictating how we transact business. So, you make the best of it.

To transact business today, we're expected to look and sound as professional, on-screen as we do in-person. Sounds simple enough, right? Just push "record" on your smartphone and talk. Log into a Zoom call and do business with the Brady Bunch. Nothing to it, right? Wrong! Actually, there's a whole lot to it and what you don't know about, scripting, on-screen, presenting, sound, lighting, and cameras… you just DON'T KNOW. This can seriously hurt you, damage your reputation, and cost business opportunities. The dollars and hours lost are bad enough, but these poor-quality videos also damage your reputation. Yikes! Accordion nightmares.

Oh, Brother! Another Learning Curve?

It was the winter of 2007. I was in my photography studio and about to step in front of a professional video camera. It was the first time I "formally" talked to a lens. I was producing a promotional video for my proprietary EPS Portraits service. I had the lighting nailed down. No surprise there, I was a lighting expert who taught other professional photographers. I had a wireless mic clipped to my lapel. Check. I have my bullet points to talk from. Check. I can do this. No sweat. TAKE ONE!

I recorded a few versions while thinking, "Wow. I'm struggling a bit with the phrasing, and... why can't I remember my lines? I delivered this same message at my networking group just a few days ago. Why am I struggling with it today?" I began to sweat.

Time to watch the replay. "Oh... I was wrong. I wasn't struggling a BIT. This is a total train wreck! Incongruent body language, confusing message, flat delivery, my words were all jumbled. What's that banging noise? Oh, I was bumping the microphone." Even though there was no one in the studio with me, I felt totally embarrassed watching the playbacks.

Talking WITH another person while being captured by a video camera is relatively easy. However, talking TO a camera is a whole different world. Horrified by the playback, I erased the footage. I swore I would never try this again. I went home to take a shower. I was so incredibly stressed over this experience I was drenched in sweat. I sweat during an intense workout — on a hot summer day! — this was the middle of winter. The studio was cool and quiet. The furnace was off, and I was alone. How could I have been that nervous? How could I be that bad on camera?

Jared, You Can't Guide Clients to Do What You Can't Do

I've made several career shifts over the years. From high-end product photography to proprietary business portraits, to response marketing, and now to promotional video production with presentation coaching. Today, I am required to have the ability to coach my clients through the process of making engaging videos. They must look and sound professional on-screen. They must be totally congruent with their message and offer!

I asked myself on that winter day in 2007, "How can I be an effective coach if I cannot do what I am asking others to do?" How could I guide others to develop their on-screen competence when I could not develop my own? The answer was... I could not, so I fixed it! I worked diligently on how to move and how to alter my phrasing and tonality. I focused on making my delivery congruent with the messages I shared. This instant replay is a fabulous bio-feedback tool to see those micro expressions! It's been a few years... I now look and sound pretty natural when I engage in this very unnatural communication medium.

Guiding People through this Transformational Change is Terrific Fun!

As our 42nd U.S. President was fond of saying, "I feel your pain." I can still remember that horrible sinking feeling of reviewing my first video takes... like it was yesterday. I believe that's why I empathize with my clients and make their journey along the business video path as simple, easy, and fun as possible!

I call the unwanted results in one's video "Digital Static™." It's those distracting elements within a video that cause a perfect prospect to click off before they get to the offer. What a shame because your offer is exactly what that person needs! My current day "why" — and the reason that I am here — is to guide people to "Delete the Digital Static™" from their business videos.

Kelly's Success Story:

Kelly is an Entrepreneurial Couples' Coach. She was presented with the opportunity to speak in front of an association comprised of audience members who are her perfect prospects. She was required to submit a video explaining her unique platform and coaching opportunities. Kelly shared her self-produced video with Gail Brown of Engaging Speakers. Gail referred Kelly to me.

Kelly's self-produced video was loaded with pretty common Digital Static™ elements like: bad sound, bad lighting, no script, fast pace rambling presentation, redundant statements, no call to action, and a runtime that was too long. I worked with Kelly to improve her messaging and on-screen presence. We produced a new promo video. As a result, she's been invited to more stages and has won new clients.

To view Kelly's "Before and After" video, visit: https://l.ead.me/bcbnsr

Louie's Success Story:

Louie is a "keynote speaker" and "speak-to-sell presenter." His on-stage presence is brilliant! Unfortunately, a good deal of that brilliance was initially disrupted by Digital Static™ when Louie began making presentations on-screen. I'm proud to say that we've deleted that Digital Static™. Louie's brilliance can now shine through on handheld devices and computer screens across the globe.

To see and hear Louie's success story video, visit: https://l.ead.me/bcbnja

Steve's Success Story:

An extraordinary inspirational speaker, author, and sales trainer, Steve Beck has been on corporate stages across the country for decades. In post-recession years, major corporations have scaled back on the number of "outside speakers" hired. Rather than 10 or 12 annually, it's now only two or three per year. Wanting to be in that top tier category, Steve realized that having superb skill sets wasn't enough. So we had a brainstorming session to determine how we might leverage the power of video to keep him among the elite presenters who are brought back year after year.

We decided to use, what I call, the Touch Point Video™ model. We've been emailing Steve's 60 second-ish "Beck Shorts" videos every morning for the past seven years to Steve's entire database. These upbeat messages are a great start to one's week. Like a friendly tap on the shoulder, "Just saying hi," and to remind clients that he's here and ready to serve them when they want him to. It's funny how people only buy from you when they want to, but not when you need the business. Go figure. :)

To see Steve's Success story, visit: https://l.ead.me/bcbndf

A Fun and Useful Video Gift for You

Thank you for reading this chapter. Now I have a "how-to video" to share with you. It will absolutely raise the bar on the production quality of your future videos to get you more business opportunities.

After guiding many people on the scripting, presenting, producing, and distribution aspects of their business videos, I've learned a few things.

1. Everyone is at a different point along their Business Video Path.

2. I've learned to listen carefully to determine where that person is along their path. As Zig Ziglar explained, "God gave us 2 ears and 1 mouth. Use them in that proportion." I love meeting people wherever they're at to provide that one thing to bring the biggest impact to their on-screen presence, right now!

3. Lastly, I've learned that if an Orthodox Introvert like me can become a competent presenter… anyone can.

I thank you for reading my story.

Jared N. Silver

Jared Silver was "shy" as a child. "Orthodox Introvert" is more accurate. It was socially acceptable for the artist/photographer to be inconspicuous... through college. However, at age 24, he was ready to follow his passion of becoming a commercial product photographer. This required stepping into the spotlight to bring clients to the door. Armed with basic sales psychology, a stunning portfolio, and promotional materials, he made sales calls. During the 1980s and '90s, Jared enjoyed a recurring six-figure income. AT&T, Abbott Labs, Brunswick Corp., Cuisineware, Kitchens of Sara Lee, Motorola, Washburn Guitars, Solo Cup Co., and Xerox were among his clients. Aside from ongoing sales and follow-up activities, Jared maintained his "behind the camera disposition."

Jump ahead 18 years. Sales copywriting, proprietary business portrait services, and video production are the latest offerings. With internet bandwidth expanding exponentially, Jared bravely steps in front of the video camera to produce online marketing videos. He plans to guide others in doing the same. The initial results? Disastrous! Horrible on screen! These videos were destroyed!

Jared diligently led his Video Clone™ from typical to terrific to brilliant... to get more business. He now guides others to do the same. His "Four Cornerstones of Effective Business Video" are shared at numerous networking events. He is also a recurring presenter for the Small Business Administration.

Jared has been featured on WGN and multiple podcasts. He has crewed on video interviews of business celebrities, including the inspirational Zig Ziglar, Robert Kiyosaki (Rich Dad Poor Dad), and Michael Gerber (The E-Myth). He has produced promotional videos and photos for numerous speakers, authors from Engaging Speakers, and NSA, including "Millionaire Maker" Robert G. Allen.

Jared N. Silver
At A Glance Marketing
Barrington, IL
847-774-9568
Jared@AtAGlanceMarketing.com
AtaGlanceMarketing.com

Nix the Nostril-Damus

How to boost your On-Screen Video Presence right now!

- What is Digital Static™?

- Why is it so damaging?

- How to Delete Digital Static™ so you can get more business?

In this popular module, from my online course, called "Nix the Nostril-Damus" I will show you how to eliminate some of the most common Digital Static™ issues that kill the effectiveness of the videos we see every day. The more Digital Static™ you delete from your videos, the more engaging you will become and the more business opportunities you will get. Enjoy the show!

https://l.ead.me/bcbnYU

Sheila Anna Vaske

Powerful Mind. Powerful Soul.

"What your mind gives power to; has power over you."

These were the words that ultimately changed my life. There are a few stories that I will share with you on how I healed myself twice medically and how I came back after losing my business in this story. My first story begins with the time when I was a freshman in high school. My health teacher started the class with that particular quote and went on to talk about the power of the mind and how we can heal ourselves and change our lives all through the way we program and think in our own minds.

This was fascinating to me for many reasons. However, one of the main reasons at that time was that at the age of 11, I was diagnosed with a very rare disease called "scleroderma." At the time, it was extremely rare, and even more so to get it as a child. You could say the odds of getting this as a child were like winning Powerball twice in your lifetime.

It all started when I was having trouble with my right index finger for about a year or so. My finger was very swollen and felt like it was broken and/or bruised. However, a few months later, it became very tight, and I could not bend it or make a fist with my hand any longer. Soon after that, my entire right arm became very skinny, shiny (it looked badly burned), and I lost all the hair on my arm. My mother took me to many doctors and specialists. However, nobody could figure out what was wrong with me. Our last doctor said to my mother… "We cannot figure out what she has, but what I can tell you is that whatever it is, she will not live long."

Can you imagine hearing that about your child? Well, that certainly sparked her to talk about it with others. This led her to take me to Boston Children's Hospital for a diagnosis. It took months to get in. However, on the very first day of arriving at the hospital, I was seen by many doctors and specialists. They decided, as a whole, to diagnose me with scleroderma. Based on this being so rare, I had become a case study for Boston Children's Hospital at 11 years old. The doctors did say that I would never have function of my right arm or hand ever again. I would also need to learn to be left-handed. They also gave me a diagnosis of five years to live.

At the time, I had accepted this diagnosis. I learned to do as much as I could with my left hand and just accept what it was. I was always a positive person, even as a child, but the day my health teacher said those words I mentioned in my opening statement changed my life instantly. He talked about how powerful our mind is and how we can change our lives for the better or for the worst, by the thoughts we allow ourselves to think and what we create in our minds. We can limit ourselves on what we can achieve, or we can choose to exceed in anything we want to do, become or receive, even when others may deem it as IMPOSSIBLE. All of this can be done by using and training the power of our minds. From that day forward, I made a decision. That decision was that I would *no longer* give this disease any of my attention ever again.

My healing journey began immediately! I started by squeezing a tennis ball every single day until I could make a closed fist and joined a gym. I was 14, and I went to the gym and worked out every single day. I also began working... in fact, I ended up working three jobs in high school. Funny enough, before I started my mindful healing, many people would come up to me and ask if I had been burned in a fire because the disease caused my arm to look shiny and scarred. However, once I stopped giving it any attention and believed that I would no longer accept the diagnosis I was given, the scarring and shininess began to go away. People didn't ask that question anymore. I told myself and believed that I would live and move on to live a long, fulfilling life, just like everybody else. My arm now began looking amazing because of the skin tightening around all my joints. I looked like I was a gym rat and worked out all the time! Since that happened, I needed to work on my left arm to make sure it could look just like my right arm! (imagine!) That being said, I have maintained function and done all things possible ever since. Most people still do acknowledge my arm, but now, it's in a positive way because it looks like I have worked out for a living!

Since I was a little girl, I knew I was different. I believe we all are special. I think we should learn to embrace that! I know today's world can challenge us and make it very hard to be unique, special, authentic, and genuine. However, I believe we need to embrace and embody the great qualities we have within us and use them to our strongest abilities. Our minds can change the trajectory of our lives in every aspect, including our mental, physical, spiritual, and financial health.

Our mind affects our soul, which in turn radiates the energy we project onto others. For example… Did you ever wake up in a bad mood one day? What happens? Let me guess… Your whole day seems to go terribly. It seems like nothing can go right, and everything continues to go wrong. You catch every red light. A bill comes in the mail you didn't expect. If you're a student, you forgot your homework. If you are a parent, your kids are out of line all day long, and they are exhausting you. Whatever the case may be, it just seems like nothing can go your way. When you have these types of days, it is usually the negative energy that you are putting out into the universe.

Now, think of another example. You wake up very happy one day, and everything seems to be amazing. People are smiling at you everywhere you go, perhaps even complimenting you. You might get an unexpected check in the mail, or money somehow appears for you. You seem to catch every green light, your grades may be amazing, your children are full of love and laughter that day, etc.

Again, the mind controls the soul, which controls the energy we radiate… GOOD or BAD.

Here is another example... Do you ever get a day where suddenly you think of somebody you haven't spoken with in a while? They might just cross your mind, or maybe you think of a time you shared and reminisced about that instance or time in your mind. Those thoughts also create feelings, such as laughter, love, etc.... Then all of a sudden, out of nowhere... they reach out to you! Whether it's through a call, text, social media, or a picture on your phone... they APPEAR!

This is proof that once again, the power of your mind and the thoughts that run through it radiate like a magnet. It is an invisible energy that radiates to that person you're thinking of. Think about this. If that particular energy can radiate to that person from one state or country to another, imagine what it can do for *you* within *your own self* in your *own body*.

> *"What you think, you become. What you feel, you attract.*
> *What you imagine, you create."*
>
> —Buddha

Think about how powerful those words are. Take a moment to reflect on them.

The next story of my personal healing journey happened very recently. I want to share how I healed myself. It was once again with the power of my mind. In 2020, I had a company that meant the absolute world to me. It has been my dream to inspire, motivate, protect, and heal as many people as I possibly can. If you haven't noticed yet, I am also very spiritual. I spent many years (nine to be exact) creating an inspirational jewelry and accessories company. They were intended to inspire, motivate, protect, and heal as many people as possible through my own creations.

My dream was to grow the company on a global level. I wanted to be in every store I could possibly be in. We were almost there! I was preparing another line with buyers interested throughout the United States. At this time, I had been published in three best-selling magazines, two years in a row as a featured woman for International Women's Day, I had made it on HSN, and I also made it on the only TV shopping network in Canada. In fact, I even sold out of three of the items that we aired and discussed that evening. We did so well that by the time I was heading to the airport, they had placed another order. However, just before we were ready to launch to some major retailers in the United States, COVID and the pandemic happened. That being said, I could not sustain myself. I lost my company. In my world, it felt like I had lost everything! I must say I never grieved in my life, until this time. I have been through a lot in my life, as I'm sure we all have. I just never personally grieved over any of them until then. This, to me, was like losing a child. I could not understand what and why this was happening!

Before the loss, I was super healthy and thriving! I ran four to five miles a day, managed my business, felt amazing, and fell in love. Life was GREAT! All until this happened! About a month later, I contracted COVID. Because of the stress I was under, and since scleroderma is an autoimmune disorder, I became very ill. My body went through what was called a "Leukemoid Reaction." This meant that I showed every sign and symptom of leukemia. I went to see an oncologist, who ran tests to see what form of leukemia I had. This was on March 19th, 2021. I was scheduled to go back on March 29th for my treatment plan moving forward. However, I **made a decision** that day, just like the one I made when I was 14. I would walk in on the 29th and be another **"medical miracle."** I refused to accept what I was being diagnosed with and decided I would do whatever it takes to show up on the 29th free from any disease and would prove that my blood work would come back perfectly NORMAL. Trust me. This has never happened in my whole life!

That being said, I did A LOT of research, changed my diet, researched supplements to take, meditated, prayed, and journaled. I did all I could do and made up my mind and manifested, becoming another medical miracle! When I walked in on March 29th, they took another blood test... My blood work was **PERFECT!** All of the tests to figure out what type of leukemia I had came back negative. This was how we learned it was just a type of reaction my body went through because of the autoimmune disease I have.

I would be lying if I told you that this was easy… In fact, it was and still is, FAR FROM IT! It is October 2021 as I write this. I am still considered a long hauler from COVID. However, I am improving every day and every week… I take it one day at a time and do the best I can.

I am continuously working towards healing myself, not just physically but mostly mentally and spiritually. When I went through that moment of grieving, I lost my sense of self and what I stood for. I lost who I was and what my purpose was. Once again, I needed to make a decision. The question was and is, "How will I overcome this and change my life. Who will I become now?"

I realized that the passion that lived inside my soul *still* lives there today. It is still the passion and calling to inspire others to be the best versions of themselves. I want to shine my light wherever I go and whenever I can.

I began to give my fears and problems to God once again and prayed hard. With prayer also must come faith and trust. This means letting go and letting God.

Letting Go and letting God led me to an introduction with the creator of this book, which led me to writing this book! For the last 18 years, I have been saying I would and wanted to write a book! Here we are! I have also created inspirational quote cards with exercises on them and a journal that allows you to express how those exercises worked for you.

I have again realized that I do not need jewelry or accessories to inspire others. The nine years I worked so hard on that business, I learned that I inspired people on my own. This is who I am at my core. I realized that I can do that in many ways. Here I am today doing exactly that!

Once we realize that, life is just a journey. We are all trying to get somewhere and be the happiest we can be. Keep in mind that happiness isn't the same for everyone. It comes in many forms for many people. The challenge is, what does it mean for us personally? What do we need to find out? It is **what** and **who** we are at the core of ourselves. What does our soul crave, and how does our mind think? How can we put that together and change our lives for the better? Better than that, how can we also serve others and change their lives for the better? Imagine a world where everyone was respectful and kind to everyone.

The purpose and mission of this book is to tell you my story, my healing, and my passion.

You can get started on changing your life with my inspirational cards, exercises, and journal, by visiting my website at www.PowerfulMindPowerfulSoul.com.

It has also been my dream and mission to inspire others through sharing my story on stage. I am ready and available to do so through speaking engagements. I especially want to reach our younger generation and teach them that all things are possible through the power of their mind, just as it was for me.

Sheila Anna Vaske

Sheila Anna Vaske was born and raised in Rhode Island. After moving 29 times, she finally resides in sunny Florida. In addition to being a proud mom of two daughters, she is also an entrepreneur at heart. Business is not the only passion that drives her, however. In fact, most would describe Sheila (including Sheila herself) as creative, intuitive, and passionate. She is also considered to be a healer and empath. The power of the mind and soul have driven her to rise above during the most difficult times along her journey. Her lessons are intended to inspire and drive others to also do the same in all facets of their life.

Her last company was guided to her spiritually. She dedicated nine years of her life to growing it into an inspirational brand of jewelry and accessories, before losing it to COVID in 2020.

However, one thing she did not lose was her passion and drive to continue to inspire and motivate others to become the best versions of themselves. Through her own experiences, Sheila shares how she has healed herself physically, mentally, spiritually, and financially.

Sheila is extremely passionate about educating others on how to use the power of their mind and how to enable them to implement that power themselves to heal their life, health, body, and spirit, as well as their careers.

Sheila has also been published in three bestselling magazines.

- Where Women Create — Jan/Feb/Mar 2019 Edition

- Where Women Create Work — "A Passion for Success" Spring Edition 2019 — Highlighted as one of 18 Women to be featured for International Women's Day

- Where Women Create Work — "Women Working for a Stronger America" Annual Edition 2020 — Featured as one of the Women

Sheila Anna Vaske
Powerful Mind Powerful Soul
Seminole, FL
401-248-1512
Sheila@sheilavaske.com
www.PowerfulMindPowerfulSoul.com

Take Your MIND and SOUL to the Gym Every Day!

Each morning we wake up is another gift and opportunity to begin healing your life with the power of your mind and soul. It begins with the proper tools, taking the first step, and staying consistent through repetition.

What's included:

- A 33 Inspirational Card Deck of quotes and daily exercises to do throughout your day.

- A 50 Page Journal. This journal prompts you on the card you pulled. Your "quote and exercises of the day," along with additional pages to journal any other thoughts and feelings you may have encountered.

- A beautiful, black gel pen in a velvet pouch. (FREE)

Use code: IAMREADY and receive all three tools for only $44 (*$56 Retail Value*)

Scan our QR Code or visit our website at www.PowerfulMindPowerfulSoul.com

Sairan Aqrawi

The Truth of "American Dream"

It is December 3, 1997, 5 am, cold and dark in Kurdistan. I am waiting for the driver to pick me up. I fight back tears in front of my father, who is standing near the front door. I am leaving my parents and my siblings. My father is wondering if there is a chance that I could change my mind. He is battling stage 4 cancer.

As much as it hurts to leave, I face too great a risk to stay. I am counting on meeting the best me in the years ahead.

The Start...

I am forced to leave Northern Iraq because of my work for U.S. aid groups. Thousands, like myself who worked for Non-Government Organizations (NGOs), were at risk of retaliation by the Iraqi regime. The State Department received presidential approval to implement a voluntary evacuation. I now have to leave my country, family, and roots and move to the United States.

I am in my twenties. With only 700 dollars but millions of dreams, I am heading to the unknown. First stop the border, Turkey, and then Guam. Yes, Guam.

It is a long-distance between Iraq and Guam, with nearly 6,300 miles of air travel. Plenty of time for fears to develop along the way.

Whether you have moved to the USA because you chose to or you were forced to, my story is for you.

Guam was like paradise because I grew up in a war zone. Everything was calmer, safer, and we had more freedom. I knew how to speak English, which qualified me to help others at the military camp in Guam. I was helping those who were less fortunate adapt to the new environment that we were all heading to. I personally would love to relive that Guam experience. I didn't feel as if I was a stranger at all. We were all welcomed. The way we were treated by the military staff and the conditions we were living in were amazing. We were considered political asylees in Guam. We had high expectations of the States. We thought the same lifestyle and amazing support we were receiving in Guam from the military staff was going to be the same in the United States.

However, the palm trees in Guam with the relaxing, safe memories were not the same when we arrived in the United States.

I was young and single. I thought when I finally arrived to the U.S., the first person I would see at the airport would be Kevin Costner or at least someone who looked like him with gray eyes. Instead, it was racism and stereotyping that still exists today.

Despite that rocky beginning, I was able to make my American dream come true as I discovered three keys to making it work. Since then, I've coached countless new international teams, students, families, and individuals who come to the states. I will share my three secrets so you can achieve your American dream.

"Move away from your country and seek the best version of yourself.
Your new identity will come out polished and unique."

Secret Number 1: Embrace the Positive Side of the New Culture

Be open to all possibilities. Don't assume that the unknown is bad for you. We can always pick the positive seed and stay away from the bad ones.

If you don't embrace the new culture, you will still be a prisoner of your old beliefs and live in a bubble that will prevent you from progressing in many ways.

The solution is to embrace the new culture, and you will be set free.

Lubna came from the Middle East. She was confused and not able to absorb the new culture. This made her advancement here very challenging. Serving as her mentor, I was able to coach her six months after her arrival. Focusing first on this principle with her. She understood if she couldn't master this tool, she would miss many opportunities for progress that would come her way in the United States.

She is now a full-time teacher living in peace and harmony with her husband and two children. Not only is she more settled in her life, but she embraces the positive side of the different cultures. She is thinking of opening a business with her husband. I recently called her to see how far she is in her continued progress. I asked her, "Where are you now?" She replied, "I am finally home... and that's exactly what you want to feel... home... safe... and loved."

"You might plant your seeds in Asia, but you might end up harvesting them in Canada! The seeds are already on the ground, and we all live in the same globe. Move from where you live. There is excitement waiting for you far away."

Secret Number 2: Finding Your New Identity

Find what makes you unique in your new community. This doesn't mean that you have to become a new person. The unique personalities and cultures from all over the world are part of what makes America such a unique place.

You may no longer have a close physical connection to many things you enjoyed doing, such as playing a certain sport or taking part in traditions. However, there are still sports and traditions here for you to learn and let become a part of you. Find things here that you want to bring into your life.

This process takes many months, if not years. It can be exciting for some and make others want to curl up in bed. I encourage you to view it as a chance to re-invent yourself into who you always wanted to be. In America, you have the freedom to be who you want. You can do things that you never thought possible. People here want to see you succeed.

If you don't find your identity, you will not open up to all of the wonderful new things in your new home. Refusing to enjoy parts of the culture here will only hold you back from reaching your full potential. It may not be comfortable for you to move out of your comfort zone like this. However, it is necessary in order to get the full experience. You may need to leave some things behind to be able to look forward to what the future has in store for you.

Who you are as a person doesn't have to change. You just have to identify as an immigrant who is living in America and is going to do their best. Then you are on your way to the American dream! Stay true to yourself and your personal beliefs, work hard, and be kind. *Your identity will be a good one.*

I met Alan, who came from Russia. He asked me to coach him for six months. He was a very smart engineer. He came here with a piece of paper called a degree. He thought that all doors would be open for him and life would be easy. We had our coaching around setting goals, making an impact, and leaving our old, negative beliefs behind. He realized that if he didn't get clear on his destination, he would waste all of his time thinking about his past achievement in Russia and not be able to pursue the new personal improvement that lay in front of him here. Once his perspective changed, he landed his dream job, had plans to buy a house, and he and his wife are expecting their second child. He not only experienced his success in the U.S., but he also found his new identity here.

"The minute you give yourself permission to change, the next minute, opportunities will knock at your door!"

Secret Number 3: Have Fun During the Transition and Achieve a Balanced Life

Transitioning into a different lifestyle in a new place makes it hard to focus on all of the good things. You can be working hard at a job and doing good work. However, if you are not enjoying it, you are missing out on a large part of what living in America is all about.

Americans love to have fun, and that includes those who work all of the time. To have a long and happy life, take time to enjoy it.

Achieving success here does take a lot of hard work. This is especially true if you are not starting with a lot of money and an advanced education. At the start, it will be especially difficult to see how you could one day have time to stop and enjoy the fruits of your labor. It is important not to lose sight of why you are doing this and not to let this opportunity slip away from you.

Remember, you are already here. Why not make the best of it? Like Edward de Bono said, "America is not just a country. It is an idea." I followed these principles from the day I arrived in Guam. It did wonders for my work and personal life. It works for me and it works for my clients.

I started coaching Zara in this particular area. She moved from Ghana and was raised by a military father. She saw every change here as a difficult task that she could not finish. I emphasized the importance of having fun during her transition to the U.S. She started adding exciting activities to her daily life, besides working and raising three children by herself. I showed her the importance of having a good time while still taking work and progress in your life seriously. Zara is now finishing her master's degree in engineering. Her children are also doing very well in school. She is active in two women empowerment groups. She found her way here through self-development while having a good time.

"Travel away... settle away... your best stories reside away... everything that's new will take your mind away..."

Those outside America often think of the American Dream as something out of a movie.

The American dream is NOT:

- Fancy vacations with a maxed-out credit card.
- Faking happy faces in Instagram pictures at the beach.
- Posing in front of the Congress.

- Buying expensive brands and trendy clothes.
- Showing up at events with a different boy/girlfriend each time to look cool.
- Being a part of the influential political party.
- Using English words in your conversation with your own people to impress them.

Instead, I see... a series of small enjoyments that develop the big dream with many vivid colors.

The American dream IS:

- Seeing the magic in watching the fireworks on July 4th every year.
- Counting down at Times Square on New Year's Eve.
- Having privacy in your house.
- Having the freedom not to share your personal life with a family relative.
- Being able to hang out in simple jeans and no makeup.
- Having the space and right to enjoy your own company.
- Living in your dream house that gets decorated many times throughout the year.
- Volunteering to help those who don't even speak your language.
- Being able to explore education even while you are working.
- Gaining the courage to open any business you would have loved to have your entire life.
- Choosing your partner without other people judging.
- Traveling just to explore, not to show up.
- Feeling safe while walking down the street.
- Coexisting with others in this land.

- Being able to greet others on the street or the elevator without really knowing them.

- Keeping your childrens' private lives inside your home circle.

- Not having a reason to ask how much your spouse makes at work.

- Going back to school to earn your Ph.D. even though you just turned 65.

- Having the ability to make all the pictures on your vision board a reality.

- Being able to tell noisy people to stop asking personal questions and showing them the door.

- Allowing you to stay focused in order to make things happen.

- Supporting different human rights groups asking for donations to help others around the world.

- Being surrounded by strong parents who educate others on social media for safe driving and educate about drug abuse, while grieving their own loss.

- Achieving recognition for your hard work without calling in a favor from a relative.

- Smiling and giving compliments about other people's clothes, children, cars, and shoes does not make you look weird.

- Laughing and sharing stores with other parents at your child's school activities.

- Seeing people who do not celebrate Christmas chip in to donate their time to the Salvation Army and ring the bell outside of stores.

- Being a part of this amazing land.

"Work hard on your American dream…
there are many hidden diamonds in muddy ways."

Voices of Truth in My Life in the U.S.

- Here my endless love story was born.

- Here the world welcomed another falcon, my son Baz.

- Here I brought my Hana, who added an amazing smell to the universe.

- Here I became able to be who I wanted to be, since I was 13.

- Here I learned that being a smart engineer and solving equations does not make you a master.

- Here dreams are allowed without penalties.

- Here you can find your own U.S. (Unique Skills) and grow in the big U.S. (United States). It won't always be a smooth path, there will be some disappointment and backstepping, but also applause and achievements.

- Here while you are building your best, you will see the same people who used to laugh at your accent a couple of years ago now desperately searching you on the web and wondering how you become an entrepreneur all of a sudden.

Your list may be different from mine, which is why the American Dream is open to everyone who comes here. My wish for you is to remember the three secrets:

1. Embrace the new culture.

2. Find your new identity.

3. Have fun during the transition and achieve a balanced life.

The result is a better version of YOU!

Sairan Aqrawi

Sairan Aqrawi is the CEO of International Transition Expert, a successful transformation coach, an engaging speaker, a knowledgeable and attentive mentor, a co-author of a bestselling book, and so much more!

A humble yet professional leader, Sairan has the knowledge and motivation to help you live your best life. Her goal is to leverage your strengths and empower you to transform your life, finding your true happiness, and making you feel at home wherever you are.

Sairan is an ACC Associate Certified Coach and a distinguished mentor at George Washington University's Women in Engineering (WiE) and Women in Technology (WiT). With over two decades of experience in coaching and mentoring international teams, families, individuals, and college students, Sairan has built a business founded on real-life experience, extensive knowledge, and a passion to help others like you accomplish the American Dream!

Sairan has helped hundreds of individuals transitioning to the United States struggling with fear, confusion, culture shock, language barriers, and isolation. She makes you feel safe and have fun, while adapting to a new culture. She is ready to help you find profitable work that fits your passion and lifestyle.

Sairan is intelligent, bold, and has a compelling sense of humor and an infectious presence. Her ability to connect with and relate to the audience allows her to engage and transform the room.

Sairan's journey to the United States has inspired her desire to help others accomplish the American Dream. As a native Kurdish from Iraq, she came to the United States over 20 years ago. She brings 30 years of corporate experience in engineering and team building. She is an expert problem solver with a love for teaching. Sairan believes that becoming a civil engineer has allowed her to get where she is today and find her true passion.

Sairan Aqrawi
International Transition Expert
703-622-7459
Info@InternationalTransitionExpert.com
www.InternationalTransitionExpert.com

Feel Alone? Like You Don't Belong? How Do You Make the Most of the American Dream?

Moving to the U.S. presents challenges that you may not feel prepared for. I felt the same way when I first immigrated over 20 years ago. Since then, I've built a life beyond my dreams and now coach others on how to unlock their own American Dream.

If you're ready to overcome all the major obstacles you might face when transitioning to the United States, download my free guide: Seven Keys to Live your American Dream!

American dreams are about being and feeling alive — in your work, play, and family life. Don't live your past here — live your future!

www.InternationalTransitionExpert.com

Christine Bright

Winning the Parenting Game

When I was a little girl, there was a lot of yelling in my home. It is a typical occurrence in abusive homes. I was used to it. So much so, yelling is a behavior I brought into my parenting. I will painfully admit that I even threw things a few times. I didn't realize it was an issue until I witnessed my four-year-old son berating one of his friends. "How dare he treat his friend like that" was my thought. My blood boiled! I was getting ready to storm outside and "Let him have it!" A sickening feeling in my gut stopped me. I suddenly realized he had learned the berating behavior from me. A sense of shame overwhelmed me. How could I have not been aware of my behavior? How could I treat my child that way? What damage had I done? Feelings of regret soon followed. Witnessing that moment was a turning point in my life. I needed to become intentional about changing this unhealthy parenting behavior.

When you grow up in an abusive home, you can go one of two ways. You can become an abuser, or you make a conscious decision to be different. When I found out I was expecting, I vowed that my child would have a better childhood than I did. How would I make my child's growing up better than mine? Well, I figured I better start reading parenting books to get some direction. Dr. James Dobson was the leading voice on parenting in church circles. My first read was his book *Dare to Discipline*. Then, when I found out I was having a boy, I read Dr. Dobson's book *Bringing Up Boys*. These books helped set me on a good path with my parenting. However, they didn't provide solutions for dealing with my anger.

Learning the Behavior Chain became a helpful tool in controlling my anger. Behaviors start with a trigger, then lead to a thought, followed by an action, which leads to a consequence. I could choose to take a moment after I was triggered to think about how to handle the situation, or I could choose to be reactionary in my responses and start yelling. For you, this is like, dah! For me, it was a mind-blowing aha! *Personality Plus* and *The Five Love Languages* were the following books I read. The information was transformational. These authors introduced a new way of thinking to me. Understanding myself and understanding others improved. As a result, my parenting choices were becoming better. I was yelling far less, and my son was flourishing!

When my son was in the 6th grade, our family had the privilege of being a pilot family for a new concept called Therapeutic Foster Care. The idea of being a big brother was exciting for my son Dalton because he wished he had a sibling. My world dramatically changed by the opportunity to become a Therapeutic Foster Parent (TFP). The TFP training was intense, and I loved it. I learned communication skills and de-escalation skills. I studied child development, brain development, and neuroplasticity. I then received boundaries training. After each night of this training, I would go home in tears.

As a victim of abuse, I realized my boundaries had not been respected or protected as a child. I wasn't allowed to say no or to have an opinion. I also experienced seeing my mom being shamed by my dad when she would hold her ground. My perception became that it was safer not to maintain boundaries somewhere along the line. It was safer to give in to someone else's will. The training taught me how to set appropriate boundaries and hold them. I knew the foster child we would be caring for would have problems resulting from boundary issues. I prioritized reading Dr. Henry Clouds' book *Boundaries* in its entirety and several other of his publications to ensure that our home was healthy in this area.

I will refer to my foster son as Eric as I continue with my story. It was a beautiful time in my life raising Dalton and Eric. Dalton and I communicated well. He felt safe to share with me because he was confident that I wouldn't lose it on him. Well, most of the time. I would still lose it occasionally. However, it forced me to learn how to apologize well! Eric, a "hot mess" of a six-year-old, stabilized quickly. During this time, I started realizing just how much words mattered. My son was easygoing. Honestly, I didn't feel the need to pay close attention to my words. Eric, on the other hand, was explosive. One word could be the difference between a calm interaction or an explosion of emotions. The idea of words having energy caught my attention. It wouldn't be until several years later that I became obsessed with studying words. However, I did notice that the spirits of these two precious boys could rise or fall depending on what I said. I started a bedtime routine of telling them the positive behaviors I had seen that day. Doing the bedtime routine was one of many strategies that brought transformation. Eric became a stable and loving boy who was successfully adopted into a caring family. My son grew into a young man who continually sees good in people.

After Eric transitioned to his adoptive family, our family relocated to Wisconsin. My career took a turn, and I became an entrepreneur. This new adventure challenged me in many areas and resulted in personal growth. At the start of my business, I hired family and friends, people I trusted, who were gifted, and could do the job well. However, I realized that their performances weren't where I thought they should be. Obviously, they needed more training. No, that was not the case. The extra training resulted in employees to start considering leaving. I shared my confusion and frustration with a fellow business owner. In their wisdom, they recommended *One Minute Manager*. This book became a voice of truth in my life. It helped me realize that I was overwhelming my staff with too much information. I also expected them to sell just like me. I took the time to read through *Personality Plus* again. I also revisited the communications skills I learned as a Therapeutic Foster Parent and incorporated them into my business. I condensed the training from three sheets of notes to one and allowed my staff to have the freedom to develop their own sales style. Being themselves without being overloaded with information propelled them into a high-performance team. Sales increased. We earned the reputation for being the preferred promotional company for Wisconsin's western and southern parts.

My career path is an interesting one. While a CEO, I was also a child care professional and family advocate. One family I worked with had three children. The middle child was very explosive and would become violent. I was confident that I could help the child become emotionally regulated. His behaviors were so disruptive that I started homeschooling him. I couldn't handle going up to the elementary school and seeing him surrounded by police anymore! While being homeschooled, he made good progress. Behavioral change happened more rapidly after studying the three parenting models suggested by his therapist. The choices were Love and Logic, Parent Management Training, and Collaborative and Proactive Solutions (CPS). I studied all three methods and found CPS to be most effective in changing behaviors.

During this time, I also was introduced to Brene Brown's research on shame. I didn't realize how easy it is to shame another person. Many times, it happens unintentionally. My obsession with how we use our words became ignited! Digging into ways to use my words better helped minimize explosive interactions with the children in my care. It also became an area of growth as a CEO. I started putting intentionality into how I approached conversations. I discovered simple word changes had a profound effect on the outcome of a conversation. For example: instead of starting a sentence with "Why did you...?" I used the phrase "I noticed." The word *why* puts a person into a defensive posture. Conversations don't go well if one of the parties feels they need to defend themselves. When a person doesn't feel defensive, it is a benefit as it dramatically improves the ability to build trust. Seeing a child change their behavior from explosive and destructive to calm and loving filled my soul with joy. I started to get a sense of my life's purpose.

Being an entrepreneur was exciting, challenging, and fun. I was proud of my company's reputation and the quality of work we did. However, as much as I enjoyed it, I had to follow the desire of my heart, which was dedicating my time fully to working with children and families. I, therefore, sold the company and focused solely on my career as a child care professional and family advocate.

I was enjoying my career as a childcare professional. Families' homes that were once chaotic were becoming peaceful. I developed language and strategies that quickly brought about behavior change without being conscious of it. One day a simple question was posed to me by a friend, and it started me on a journey I hadn't imagined. The question was, "How do you do what you do?" My answer was very profound! OK, not really because I responded with, "I don't know?" My friend followed up with a sincere statement. "It's important for you to share what you do with the world." The conversation was the catalyst to a year-long process of bringing what-I-do unconsciously into consciousness.

I was continually analyzing the conflict between parent and child. I asked a lot of what-if questions. What if a child could complete chores without being yelled at or needing a reward? What if a parent could use words in a way that eliminated "I don't know" responses and yielded truth? What if a child's "why do I have to" questions could be responded to in a teachable manner? What if someone developed strategies to address the parent and child conflict areas I have observed? Those three main areas of conflict are negative beliefs, undermining oneself, and word choices that cause defensiveness or confusion. Using my learning, training, and real-world experience of working with families, I created strategies and solved those what-if questions. This information is brought together in a teachable framework and published in the *Parenting Game Playbook*.

Yes! A Playbook. I have worked with children for over 20 years, and not one came with a manual. You will go through periods when you are winning and feel like you are losing. I know I did! I thought I had lost altogether during my divorce and becoming a single mom. But, no matter how you are feeling, the Parenting Fundamentals I will share will help you be more positive, understanding, and encouraging with your parenting choices.

Fundamental #1 is all about your stance. Every sport has a stance that sets an athlete up for success. The best stance you can take is to believe your child will succeed. If a parent's viewpoint is one of doubt, a child will lose hope. Without hope, the motivation to do better is fleeting. I understand this is a mind shift and can be tough to grasp, especially when a child exhibits challenging behaviors. However, being intentional with your stance changes how you interact with your child. Honestly, it is a parenting game-changer. For example, the my-child-may-fail approach could lead to statements like, "You didn't make your bed again. Stop being lazy!" Whereas my-child-will-succeed path leads to phrases like, "I noticed you didn't make your bed today. What's up?" I love Jentzen Franklin's powerful quote, "Speak to the fool in your child, and the fool will stand up. Speak to the King in your child, and the King will stand up." Through years of experience working with children and families, I know this is the truth.

Fundamental #2 centers around using positively charged language. I stated earlier that I became obsessed with studying words after reading Brene Brown's research. I started noticing how some words feel good, and some feel bad no matter your tone. It depends on how society uses the term. For example, the word *consequence* can mean a good thing will happen, or a bad thing will happen. In the U.S., it has a negative charge. We wouldn't say to your kids, "When you get your room cleaned, the consequence is you can have ice cream!" I guarantee you will get a funny look! The word *result*, on the other hand, "feels" more positive. The phrase "When you get your room cleaned, the result will be you can have ice cream." should get the desired action. Another common phrase that drips with negativity is, "Why did/didn't you do that?" I worked on formulating the following words for two years. "Help me understand what is/was going on with _____." All of us have a deep need to be understood. Using this phrase invites your child into a conversation in hopes of understanding them better. The language continues to prove to be a powerful way to get truth and understanding.

Fundamental #3 is understanding that your children need time and opportunity to practice behavior changes. This aha of mine came out of frustration. I was working with two boys, and the request of one parent was to work on table manners. I was facing an uphill battle. In a moment of frustration, I said, "Could you please practice putting a napkin on your lap already!" And they did! What did I say that changed their behavior? I used the word *practice* in my statement. Throughout the day, I kept using it. The boys did what I asked with no arguments. Using the word *practice* is a simple and powerful way to encourage your children towards desired behaviors.

At the time, I was reading Talent Code by Daniel Coyle. He talks about "deep practice." I am sure this is why the word *practice* came to mind. Coyle explains introducing new behaviors creates new neuro-pathways. Lasting behavior change is the result of being able to practice the new behavior over and over. The neuro-pathway fires again and again and eventually becomes ingrained in the brain. What I learned is we can get our child's compliance in the moment with threats and punishment. However, long-term change will not happen unless we set clear expectations and provide opportunities for them to practice new behaviors.

I want to be a voice of truth for you. What if you were willing to change your mindset, be intentional about choosing the words you say, and allow your children to practice the behaviors which need transformation? The result will be less parent guilt, a happier, more peaceful home, and your family will be winning!

Christine Bright

Christine Bright has over 20 years of experience working with children, parents, and families as a child care professional, family advocate, and Certified Parent and Family Coach.

Christine is an entrepreneur in her own right, starting and running a successful promotional company. In addition, she worked as a child care professional and family advocate while managing her business. Christine works one-on-one with families experiencing a wide range of problems. She also helps families navigate the steps needed to get appropriate services. Her success and positive results gave her the courage to sell her company, follow her heart, and serve families full time.

Christine honed her skills with the invaluable training she received as a Therapeutic Foster Parent. She parented her foster child to become an emotionally stable and loving person, which led to a happy adoption. This success ignited a deep, profound passion in her.

She developed and perfected her strategies while working with families using her business, child development, and behavioral psychology knowledge. With a desire to help more families, Christine then founded Parenting Game and authored her *Parenting Game Playbook*. Her unique parenting *Playbook* is transformational in assisting parents in developing communication which lessens defensiveness and fosters desirable behaviors. She also produces and hosts a TV and radio show to support parents. She delights in helping parents win by making their homes brighter and more peaceable.

As CEO of Parenting Game, her company offers support to parents, caregivers, and mentors through coaching, consulting, and training. She also partners with businesses by providing parenting support as an employee assistance program benefit.

When Christine isn't reading the latest on brain science, she enjoys the outdoors and time with family. In addition, she donates her time mentoring at-risk children through programs like Schools of Hope.

Christine Bright
Parenting Game
Madison, WI
Christine@ParentingGameWins.com
www.ParentingGameWins.com

Win at the Parenting Game Playbook

Are you frustrated by constant arguments, challenging behaviors, and strained relationships with your kids? Then, the **Parenting Playbook** is for you. I will share three powerful principles for clear and effective communication, achieving desired behaviors without threats of punishment, and building a strong bond with your child.

If you want a happier and more peaceful home today, go to www.ParentingGameWins.com to receive these powerful principles to win at the game of parenting.

Dalisia Coppersmith

The Women Who Can Change Our World

Do you believe that one brief moment can pull a thousand other moments into focus and change the course of your life? That's exactly what happened to me over a dinner I'd been waiting on for more than a year.

The pandemic caused everyone to postpone or cancel events we would never have missed otherwise. I missed my daughter's graduation from Army Ranger school. Jessica has always been tough-as-nails, but this was by far the hardest thing she had ever been through. She earned every thread on that black and gold tab — and I couldn't be there to pin it on her shoulder. Like the other Ranger parents, I was crushed. To make up for it, we planned an epic post-vaccine trip to Las Vegas to celebrate her accomplishment, as well as my own retirement from the Army Reserve. I'd given twenty-five years and my firstborn child to our nation, and we both deserved a few days of high-quality pampering. *"Vegas, here we come!"*

Unstoppable Duo

We had two goals: stunning entertainment and unforgettable dining. This would start simply with a steak dinner in our hotel restaurant, where I had been twice before. I raved about their filet mignon to the point where she agreed to order it, *medium-rare.* We toasted to both of our accomplishments with a nice red, chatting as we waited for what was sure to be the best steak she'd ever had. What *actually* landed on the table was little better than a gray slab of mystery meat. We stared at it, trying to make it seem "not that bad." It was a moment of truth.

When two hardworking women order an expensive meal that is prepared like a middle school cafeteria "special," a decision must be reached. Do we *ever-so-politely* send it back — or choke half of it down, pay the bill, and move on with our lives? Jessica and I silently agreed to just let it go. We have both seen poverty and despair in this world. I was even homeless for a short time as a child, so we realized how fortunate we were to go on vacation and dine out at all. Gratitude aside, there was another factor in play. Neither of us wanted to be labeled a *Karen* — that little nickname (insult) that threatens to keep suburban women silent forever. To be fair, the *Karens* captured on social media are not, in my opinion, assertive women. They are insecure, entitled women. Even so, *we would die before sending that steak back.*

Please understand, it's not about the steak at all. We ate truly horrendous food in the Army. We can handle it. This is about how two assertive, self-advocating women would rather pay a couple of hundred dollars for a bad meal than to simply ask the chef the make it worth their hard-earned money. **Our silent pact was the result of a lifetime of conditioning to not be "too much."** In a world that is supposedly moving toward gender parity, we had unwittingly played into the narrative against which we had fought our entire lives. Jessica earned that meal with blood, sweat, tears, hypothermia, sleep deprivation, and countless moments of utter despair in Ranger school — but none of that mattered. How many other quiet ways had we accepted social silencing and insults dressed as humor to keep us in our place?

How Did We Get Here?

Over the weeks after our trip, I journaled about other settings and relationships in my life where I'd started fading into the background so as not to displease, intimidate, or offend others. I began to see patterns that were crystal clear. My daughter and I were on the same rollercoaster ride other assertive, high-achieving women had ridden for centuries. It's the hero-to-villain story, played out in homes and schools, offices, churches, and legislatures everywhere. When trouble or failure is at the door, everyone cries for our help — and we answer. Once our strengths have accomplished their goals, they begin to tear us down.

I realized that in my career, I had always been told I was a bit too outspoken, that others were intimidated by me, and that I should try to be less "aggressive." That particular descriptor is often used in assertive women's performance reviews all over the world. However, it is rarely used for men who demonstrate the same behaviors. This curse of the strong woman also showed up in my personal life. I now enjoy a happy life with my soul mate. However, in past relationships, I was accused of being selfish for having a successful career, starting a business, pursuing degrees, and even for playing sports or going to the gym (by people who played sports and went to the gym). Love was always so — *hard*. Why did it seem far easier for other women?

The final shocking realization was that in almost every area of my life, even when I worked to soften my approach, encourage more, and criticize less, I was still cast as the villain in someone else's story. It seemed the more I changed and bent and contorted myself for those around me, the more I was held firmly in place by labels, such as *aggressive, controlling, dominating*, and *argumentative*. **How was it that I demonstrated those traits far less yet was accused of them far more frequently?** When we try to make positive changes, it becomes clear that others don't want us to change. They have cast us in their narrative a certain way and are slow to adjust our assigned roles in their lives.

I'd grown accustomed to being blamed for others' discomfort, insecurity, lack of courage, and refusal to speak up. A dose of self-awareness helped me to take responsibility for my part in interpersonal dynamics, but I took it too far. **I slowly began to make myself smaller, so that others could feel bigger.** The nice people became the silent aggressors. I gave up my personal power and effectiveness so that others could feel more confident, more powerful, more — *whatever it was they needed to feel* — as they quietly took the strong woman down. It didn't happen all the time, but it happened enough for me to finally notice the pattern.

What resulted was a mess — a big, unhealthy mess! That new dynamic didn't make anyone happy in the end. It just led to a less effective workplace, home life, or friendship, as I diminished my contributions to avoid being "too much." That had to stop. I only wish I had figured out what to do about 20 years earlier! I'd found myself in the upside-down world. I had to get back to who I really was at my core. If I could do it, then so could my daughter — but not just so we could *feel* better. The real reason we have to solve this is so we can live out our purpose and make our unique contribution. This problem isn't only ours — it's global.

Why We Resist Women Who Lead

My *anti-Karen* choice in Vegas was that one brief moment that brought a thousand other moments into focus. I realized assertive women are still allowing themselves to lose the overt and covert wars waged against us. The attacks come in many forms, but the most universal is to discredit a woman for being either too *emotional* or too *aggressive*, thereby diminishing the merits of her argument or idea. I followed the breadcrumbs of daily gender disparity from our nation's capital to the mahogany tables of boardrooms, from the cubicle farms in skyscrapers to the classrooms in our educational institutions, then all the way back to the most basic family gathering. This is where it all begins and where it must end.

I had to understand what was happening in families that translated to the global, social and professional silencing of half the world's natural leaders. I used to place the blame on religions, governments, or misogynistic businesses, but I've come to realize that **resistance to female leadership is a construct born at the dinner table, where the tribe and its rules for membership are formed.** This is where we first learn to resent women in authority — and both genders do it. When I disagree, make a request, or uphold standards, I unknowingly channel the authority figures others have resisted since they were in high chairs — *their mothers!* People expect to leave home, start successful careers, and never encounter the dinner table dynamic again. When an assertive woman shows up in their careers or in their personal lives, they subconsciously fight against her. I wondered if it was even possible to reverse a timeless dynamic like this when *no one even wants to admit that it happens right in their own homes.*

Start By Restoring One Woman

Human beings are wired to fix things, and that usually starts by trying to fix other people. However, the cliché is right — the only thing we can fix is ourselves. I had to learn how to be "me" without diminishing others or triggering their mother complex. I realized that **I could never become small enough to make others feel big enough, nor could I expect others to accept my criticism, impatience, or uncaring moments.** Years of smoothing my rough edges only resulted in me losing myself in order to be less discomforting to my "personality opposites." No one intended this outcome, but it's where years of accepting labels and blame had landed me. The only way to turn it around was to stop tiptoeing through my life and start living it again. **I needed to make a change within myself to both *less* and *more* at the same time,** to improve my interactions with others while still moving mountains.

Building Relationships at Work

After going absolutely numb for a time, believing I had no chance of being seen fairly, I regained my desire to figure this out. I started with a bit of appreciative inquiry, a method I'd applied countless times with coaching clients who were judging themselves or others too harshly. Instead of focusing on when I had gotten it wrong, I studied very closely the times I'd gotten it right — when I showed up as my best self and still offered ideas and opinions without apology. I realized there was a clear, repeatable pattern that other women could integrate into their work and home lives and that I could use far more consistently in my own. The pattern consisted of three seemingly simple strategies that are not so simple in practice.

Strategy 1: Speaking from Conscience

The first step in building relationships that value our assertive side is to master **speaking up skillfully, from conscience rather than ego.** There is a massive difference in standing for what we believe in and using our command of language to cut others in half. The latter results in resentment and broken trust. We tell ourselves that we're just making a point, but we're not. We're putting our own impatience and "rightness" over relationships. It will never work in the long run. Speaking up skillfully means managing our desire to rush everyone to our solutions without disagreement. It means breathing and listening more in order to see others' perspectives, even when we feel they are wrong. When people notice that we are building with them rather than overpowering, that is when our voices start to make a real difference.

Strategy 2: Yielding to Others

Once we dial in the right motives, timing, and presentation of our ideas, we must examine how frequently we are sharing them. Every moment of air time, every passionate demand for others' support, can rob someone else of making their contribution. Assertive women can steal the spotlight far too often for others' tolerance. When we develop a keen awareness for both the timing and frequency of our time on stage, we can implement the second step — **relational cycling, which means intentionally yielding to others.** Notice how long we are pushing versus pulling, advocating versus inquiring, and speaking versus listening. When we've been in the spotlight too long, we have to step back — *way back* — and save our air time for when we can see what others are not seeing. This is not self-silencing, but avoiding shining at others' expense.

Strategy 3: Meeting Our Moments

The third step is to plan when our expertise and talents are most critical in a project or change effort. **Managing our intensity phase lines** requires planning the intensity of our effort and debate. There are absolutely times when our ability to win must come to the forefront. Some groups barely hear a woman unless she is standing and raising her voice. Assertive women can win almost any argument that really matters to us, but we shouldn't try to. When we strive to win, we strive to make someone else lose.

Likewise, our ability to work around the clock to accomplish a goal cannot become the standard we set for our teams. Energy management allows us to be at our best when it matters most in an initiative. That can be mapped out in advance before a project even begins. I know that my voice and perspective is most useful in setting goals and strategies. The details are best left to others, so I can cycle off a bit and let them lead. My intensity is helpful again when the team starts to lose focus or forgets the big picture. The main thing I have to decide is, "What are *my moments* in this effort where the team really needs my unique contribution?" We must consciously yield to others until we know it is our time to step forward and lead.

Life Mastery for Assertive Women

The Dalai Lama said, "The world will be saved by the western woman." I say *it will be saved by women, period.* Assertive, visionary women definitely have our place in that — if we build our self-awareness, emotional intelligence, and wellness. I don't know that I'll ever see an end to the war against strong women, but I do know that I can help other women navigate it and hang onto their sanity. I can help them find their genius zone and set it loose on the world *without destroying their relationships, damaging their careers, or themselves.*

This is why I launched the Reviving Athena movement in 2021 — to *restore the women who can change our world.* We have failed to solve our most pressing problems because we have largely kept assertive women out of the decision-making process. We allow them to speak, but we aren't really listening. I want them to *be* respected and to *feel* respected so they don't shrink to the point of being silent. I want women at the table making decisions and taking actions that change the trajectory of the human race and our world.

If you are one of the women I've been talking about, you have a critical part in that. We need your voice, wherever you are, *right now* — but only if you do the internal work to stop shrinking and to show up at your best. If you've started this work, keep going. If you don't know where to start, find a coach or mentor immediately. Our future depends on women like you.

Dalisia Coppersmith

Dalisia Coppersmith is an internationally experienced speaker, executive coach, and founder of the Reviving Athena movement. Her personal mission is to "restore the women who can change our world." She specializes in dissolving unconscious resistance to women's leadership and supporting those who build inclusive organizations and vibrant communities.

With more than 25 years leading diverse teams in the military, government, and corporate sectors, Dalisia knows firsthand the triumphs and challenges of being a strong woman in a world that too often resists female leadership. She now works to restore women to the leadership roles they were meant to assume in every family, community, business, and government. She reminds us that half of the world's natural leaders are women — and we need them now more than ever!

Dalisia is also a proud wife, mother, and dog mom who loves trekking across the California desert with a good podcast that expands her heart as much as her mind. You can learn more about her keynotes, courses, coaching, free resources, and the Reviving Athena movement at: www.RevivingAthena.com.

Dalisia Coppersmith

Revive Learning & Wellness

Ridgecrest, CA

Dalisia@ReviveYourLife.US

www.RevivingAthena.com

LinkedIn.com/in/DalisiaCoppersmith

Instagram.com/Dalisia.Coppersmith

Facebook.com/groups/RevivingAthena

What Your Team Isn't Telling You

The Assertive Woman's Guide to Hacking Passive Aggression at Work

If you're an assertive, high-achieving woman, you've most likely experienced a whisper campaign against you at some point. One minute everything is fine, then suddenly — the room goes quiet when you walk in or speak up. Let's turn that around and connect with others instead!

This FREE eBook demystifies a timeless dynamic experienced by assertive women everywhere. If you made it through the last one, it's likely to happen again — unless you learn *what your team isn't telling you... and how to prevent the bait and switch of "hero to villain" at work.*

Learn what you do without knowing that you're doing it... and quick fixes for reversing a dynamic that may be slowing your success on the job.

Download your FREE copy at www.RevivingAthena.com/Resources

Angelica "Andie" Monet

My Business Optimized for My Life

The Three Minutes That Changed My Life

I was 16 years old. As I arrived home after school, I walked to the couch to rest. I was exhausted! Every day I lived in constant fear and anxiety of what would trigger my mother's anger "today." I was hopeful that today would not be a repeat of the time she tied me to a chair from my shoulders to my ankles and then beat me with whatever ropes and kitchen utensils she could find in her blind and uncontrollable fury. As if that wasn't enough, she cut off my long-chestnut hair with rusty kitchen scissors. I'm still traumatized by that and many other episodes like this.

As I lay on the couch, I just started to relax. But in an instant, I tightened up. I could hear my mom's high heels clicking towards the front door. While I wished I could melt into the couch so she would avoid me, I wasn't lucky that day. I heard her coming closer. The next three minutes were like a bad and surreal nightmare. She pulled me by my hair, across the living room floor, into the hallway, and towards the front door. She screamed. "I don't want to be your mother anymore. I'm done." With one final pull and a kick, she slammed the door behind me. All I could do was beat on the door, cry, scream and beg her to let me back in.

By nightfall, my reality set in like the coldness that rises in the evenings. My hands were bloody and bruised. My hair was coming out in chunks. My shirt was wet from wiping my nose because I had nothing else. I was now homeless. After thousands of thoughts, fears, and questions, my first step was to just find someplace warm and dry to sleep. Without luck, I ended up under her deck at the water's edge, hoping the tide would not come in before I woke. I didn't really sleep much that night, but I did come to the conclusion that I needed to make some serious decisions and long-term plans. I knew my mother well enough to know there was no going back. I've seen it many times before. Her word was final, no matter how wrong she may be.

I knew that I needed money to survive. I knew that I could not financially survive without working full-time. And I also knew that I could not work full-time if I was spending all day in high school. That's when I decided that the answer to my situation was to graduate high school, start college and start my first business, all at the inexperienced age of sixteen. And that's exactly what I did.

A Handful of Challenging Years

I believe there are two critical events in a business. The first event is the startup phase, which typically involves a lot of effort and determination. I call the other event the "what next phase." This is a critical "make it or break it" time, which many business owners may not even recognize is coming.

It often falls under three areas:

- What do I do for my next growth phase?

- I'm growing, and I can grow even more. However, I know I can't sustain it without something changing.

- I can't keep up with the current growth.

I have lived and learned through each of these phases. Each one felt like a cliff that I was about to fall off. However, I also knew, thankfully, that my business would only grow as much as I did: growth of knowledge, skills, and tools. I didn't know what I didn't know yet. But I *did* know that I needed more.

I remember those stressful days, sometimes filled with tears, fear, or just emotional and physical exhaustion. But those days were all filled with questions.

I've worked many 60-to-80-hour work weeks. I love what I do. I love making my deadlines. I even love being the hero, as I call it. However, those weeks were filled with missing my children, missing a lot of sleep, and sometimes missing my sanity. What is not as easy to see is that, in that exhaustion, it can eventually lead to a "mental health day," where you can't even muster up enough focus or desire to do any work at all. The other negative side-effect is that without enough daily "detachment from work" and enough sleep, finding solutions, opportunities, or answers to challenges was not possible. Neither was it possible to have the patience or be understanding and supportive of my family.

Owning a business consists of many responsibilities. One important responsibility is business development. It involves how to "develop" the business further. Where to get new clients? How to get new clients? What new services could I offer? How can existing customers buy more? Not only are these questions constant, but it can also be exhausting. It's such a common thought that there's a common term for this: "It's like throwing spaghetti on the wall and seeing what sticks." Or another one, "It's like throwing a dart and seeing where it ends lands." Have you ever heard these before?

Cost and time are also as important as business development. How can I decrease costs when they all seem necessary and unchangeable. How could I work fewer hours without hiring someone? As my income grows, so did the need for hiring more people. But hiring people added more costs. It is also typical to lose productive work hours because of training time and learning curves. Don't you wonder how there must be an easier or faster way to accomplish tasks that seem like they should take only minutes? Even then, after adding costs that should help the business grow, profits often decrease. Once profits decrease, I was back to increasing revenue again. It was a vicious cycle, no matter how much income I made. For my clients who have any Costs of Goods/Services Sold, bringing down those costs can also be just as tricky.

Finally, there's the one most important question. How do you really actually run your business? What do corporations know that I didn't? Yikes! How do you read financial statements? Is there really something useful about them, aside from seeing the profits and using them as a tax tool? And what about KPIs? You also always hear about Key Performance Indicators (KPIs) and how corporations are all about "the numbers." Thinking of the "numbers" part of the business can feel overwhelming when you don't know "what to do" with them, what they mean, or how to fix or change them.

When Life is Perfect

Some days were filled with wondering where my next client would come from or how much money was in the bank. But other days were so joyous and amazing, especially when I really spent quality time with my children the way I wanted. Why were some days so stress-free that I wasn't worried or stressed. Most importantly, I was also more patient, understanding, and loving with my family! It's almost like the world was suspended in a peaceful perfection. Even when "fires" would come up, they wouldn't affect my happiness. How do I get to *THAT* place more often?

I am most stress-free when my business is "exploding" with revenue *and* profits, while also not adding new costs or hours to my 40-hour workweek. *That's* when my life is amazing. *That's* when and why I decided to challenge myself to create an "Optimization Plan" for my business. I wanted financial freedom and emotional joy. I also wanted to "add-back" more time in my day, which becomes more precious the older we get. My children only grow up once. I refused to let money get in the way of having quality time with them. "More money with less work hours" equals less stress and more quality time with my family.

Challenge Accepted

Here's the thing. My original background is in physics (how things work), engineering (how to design and build based on constraints and requirements), and lots of calculus and statistics. I was also "one of those kids" who wanted to figure out everything, how it worked, and how to fix things. Then add several business degrees, including accounting, economics, statistics, and finance, plus graduate school, hundreds of hours of learning and research, many thousands of dollars in education, and a lot of determination, and you end up with me, Andie Monet.

I am a natural problem solver, figure-it-out-er, and believer that the only one who can stop me is me. I knew that I could create a methodology to solve this puzzle. I was my own guinea pig, so to speak.

Please be patient with me while I share a very relevant educational point for the next two paragraphs.

Maximization is getting the most out of something that "does not exceed" specific constraints. Minimization is the opposite. You want to use as little as possible. Optimization is doing both simultaneously with multiple resources, constraints, and inputs (an example is in the next paragraph) and is often determined with the help of calculus and statistics.

For example: a business wants to *maximize* existing labor, existing systems, existing customers, and sales channels. What you want to primarily *minimize*, on the other hand, are costs. However, you may also want to minimize hours to do a certain action. For example, you may want to decrease the time it takes (by streamlining the process, automating, or optimizing systems) to bill your clients or onboard a new employee or thousands of other jobs.

Optimization Puzzle Solved

When I decided to take on my optimization challenge, I had already been optimizing specific departments and functions for over 20 years. I just was not optimizing an entire business as a whole. I have learned, implemented, developed, built, managed, and grown successful, thriving businesses for myself and others. However, those years were not just about how I grew my own business. It was also seeing, fixing, and overcoming challenges for thousands of other businesses. I knew that if anyone could figure out this puzzle, it would be me.

In an oversimplified example, it's like making dinner. There are "timing" considerations. Foods cook at different speeds and at different temperatures. Potatoes take longer to cook. Rare meat takes less time to cook. There are seasoning considerations. Pepper is great with red meat but may not be great with broccoli. How much pepper to use depends on preference and the amount of meat being cooked. What I'm trying to say is that each business has a different organizational structure, with different pieces, systems, sizes, experience levels, personality types, target market, and income levels. I look at businesses the same way. I start with "what is available for ingredients," what is the final meal that will be cooked, when it should be done, how many people will be eating, how much each person will be eating, what is the food budget, how many cooks are there to help, and how many burners and ovens will be available at what time. Then I create a strategy to get there.

Here's How It Relates to a Business:

A business has many areas that include departments, processes, advertising, marketing message, sales channels, systems, products/services, cash flow, financial statements, price points, costs-of-goods-sold, price per unit, shipping costs, documented operating procedures, current sales level, industry, geography, existing clients, and company mission and vision, to name just a handful of areas. Eventually, I make recommendations that help immediately (one day to two weeks), as well as during longer-implementation times (one month to three months).

Ultimately, my Optimization Methodology, which I call the "Nine Pillars to Explosive Profits," optimizes these three areas simultaneously:

- Explosive revenue and profits (between 25% to 300% increase) with a business tool that I created called "10-10 Business Mapping."

- No additional costs are created by teaching how, where, and why to reduce labor costs, improve productivity and efficiencies, including maximizing existing software.

- No additional working hours by teaching why, how, and where to create, analyze, and manage metrics, finances, and performance in the business.

It is also important that I teach these tools in easy-to-understand or easy-to-implement ways, even for people who don't like or are "not good with" numbers or finances. I know what is relevant (and not so relevant) with techniques, tools, effectiveness, and usefulness. Everything I teach can also be used for the life of a business. They will never be obsolete.

Three Short Business Examples

Today, over three decades after my first business, I am a Business Optimization Expert. In 35 years, I have over a thousand stories. However, I want to share at least a few that I think are really fun.

Example 1

A manufacturing client: This client had seven employees who made beauty products, like face cleansers, moisturizers, and similar items. They initially contacted me because they wanted help with preparing and securing an equipment loan to expand their manufacturing business. I told them they didn't need the loan and I would improve their business operations instead. In less than two weeks, I increased their profits by 25%. In three months, I doubled their revenue from $2 million per year to $4 million. By helping to streamline their processes, optimize their systems and reduce their costs-of-goods-sold. This also resulted in saving over $300,000 in loan interest for a loan they never needed. With the new equipment, their revenue increased again from $4 million to almost $8 million, all within 12 months.

Example 2

A construction project management firm: The owner called me to fix an Excel worksheet. I later found that it was used for monthly billing. She used multiple systems, manually entered data into ten to twenty Excel worksheets, and had several people in the billing process. Long story short, I revamped her system, streamlined her process, and automated some workflow in only 48 hours. The result was a reduced billing time from 3 ½ weeks to two days, which added more than 100 additional hours per month to get new business. By also teaching some new business development strategies, her revenue tripled in about two months.

Example 3

A publicly traded multi-billion-dollar manufacturing firm: I eliminated all overtime in one particular department within three months, saving them more than $14 million dollars per year.

Explosive Profits Planner

I wrote this chapter because my "mess" of being homeless at 16 years old was, now looking back, the beginning of my journey. It was my journey of passionately supporting businesses in a way that I never had growing up. Ultimately, I feel that I am a blessing to those not only in dark, scary places who need help but also those who are ready to really make a difference in their business and their life.

Since I believe that a business will only grow as much as its owner does, it is my great honor to offer my Explosive Profits Planner. Not only did I design this Planner to prepare you for your next explosive growth phase, but I also specifically designed it to prepare you for my 9 Pillars of Explosive Profits system when you are ready for that Program.

The Planner is powerfully designed for owners to:

- Learn the two areas that must be identified before growing a business further.
- Understand why and when your customers want to say "yes" to you.
- Confidently communicate your expertise.
- Grow your business more effectively.
- Understand your most powerful and unique ability.

- Increase sales without adding new costs.

- Have employees, contractors, and customers look forward to doing business with you.

Angelica "Andie" Monet

Angelica "Andie" Monet is a top business optimization expert and international bestselling author. She has spoken on stages with leaders like Les Brown. She has advised Fortune 500 companies, foreign and domestic governments, and over 1,000 small businesses for more than 30 years in 22 industries and ten countries.

The clients who she has worked with include:

- Monster Energy Corp
- Coca-Cola
- The United States Department of Defense
- Costco
- Walmart

- Berkshire Hathaway

- Hollywood Actors and Producers

Andie applies the same systems, insights, and elbow grease that have rebuilt nations and build Fortune 500 companies to help small business owners. Her strategic solutions and tools move businesses from "just" growth to explosive growth and profits almost overnight, while also meeting people where they are in their experience and skill level.

Abandoned by her mother at 16 years old, she started her first business, finished high school, and started college while homeless. With determination, confidence, and maybe just plain-ol' stubbornness, she now passionately focuses on creating explosive profits that do not add costs or hours to the day. This also results in a confident, empowered, and strategic business owner.

When she's not training for triathlons, saving the world, or serving at her church, Andie can be found building her non-profit to support youth leadership and entrepreneurship, hoping her adult daughter will call her, and hanging out with her son Luke, watching sci-fi and adventure movies, where they live in Lake Livingston, Texas.

Angelica "Andie" Monet
Strategic Solutions & Development International, Inc.
Texas
Andie@SSD-Intl.com
www.AndieMonet.com

Explosive Profits Planner
9 Crucial Steps to Prepare for Explosive Profits Journey

Your business will grow as successfully, as you grow yourself. So, begin your transformational journey from a "small business owner" to "corporate executive" in your own business.

This Planner will outline, guide, and support you to:

- Understand why and when your customers want to say "yes" to you.

- Present and communicate yourself as an expert in your industry.

- Grow your business more effectively, without adding new costs.

Download your Complimentary guide NOW to begin your powerful journey!

www.ExplosiveProfitsPlanner.com

Samantha Bonamassa

Accidental Entrepreneur

Fifteen years ago, if you would have talked to me about the SEC, I would have said, "Go, Gators." It is truly unbelievable how things have changed since then. I am now over three and half years into owning and operating Coast to Coast Compliance, a consulting firm I founded, after a series of events that led to me becoming an "Accidental Entrepreneur."

Coast to Coast Compliance focuses on providing customized and flexible outsourced compliance solutions for investment advisers, alternative asset managers (private equity funds, hedge funds, real estate funds, venture capital funds, etc.), broker-dealers, and other financial services organizations with assets under management ranging from several hundred million to several billion dollars. In short, for anyone not familiar with the world of securities compliance and financial regulations, I assist clients with SEC, ERA, and state registrations, develop customized compliance programs, and conduct as-needed compliance testing, training, and program reviews to ensure that they stay in compliance and stay out of trouble with the SEC and other financial security regulators.

Coast to Coast Compliance is not your traditional compliance consulting firm and I am not your typical compliance consultant. Armed with unique insight *(and what some have called "contagious enthusiasm")*, I provide proactive, comprehensive, and independent compliance solutions to empower a strong culture of compliance and meaningfully impact my clients' businesses. I take the chaos out of compliance and deliver value by freeing up my clients' internal resources, so that they can focus on other aspects of their business, while I focus on the regulatory and compliance functions they would like to outsource.

The trajectory of my personal, educational, and professional experiences has shaped who I am and how I got where I am today. To help paint this picture, I need to briefly backtrack to my formative years in Florida. At a very young age, I was taught the importance of commitment and discipline and applied those values to all of my passions. I participated in a variety of sports throughout my childhood and adolescence. At the age of 11, after a few years of practicing karate, I took home a national championship title.

When I was a 14-year-old high school sophomore, I began taking classes to receive college credit through a dual enrollment program. Thankfully, I was still able to participate in the traditional high school experience by playing varsity sports, attending homecoming dances and proms, etc., and working various part-time jobs, all while spending my afternoons and weekends driving to the local college in my town. I learned the importance of hard work, dedication, and hustle at a young age. Ever since then, these values have remained a common theme throughout my life.

I expedited my education and graduated with my associate's degree a couple of weeks before my high school graduation. At the age of 17, I entered the University of Florida as a junior. While my high school experience was quite traditional, my college experience was anything but. Nonetheless, I had a fantastic time at the University of Florida and thoroughly enjoyed being a Florida Gator, albeit for only two years. It didn't hurt that we won several national championships during my time at UF, not that I had anything to do with them, but Gainesville was buzzing, and it made for a great college experience.

When I graduated with my bachelor's degree at the age of 19, I knew I wanted to attend law school. I also realized the likelihood of not being taken seriously, because if I went to law school immediately, I would have wound up a 21-year old attorney. Instead, I stayed in Gainesville, Florida, for the next three years and churned out 100-hour weeks, working a full-time salaried day job, as well as bartending in the evenings and on weekends.

After this experience, I felt invigorated and eager for a change. I was ready to apply for and attend law school, so I enrolled at Ave Maria School of Law in Naples, Florida. I quickly learned that I was at least 50 years too young and a few million dollars too poor to live in Naples. However, it was one of the best times of my life. I thoroughly enjoyed law school and made the absolute most of it. I was fortunate to surround myself with amazing people, who would turn out to be lifelong friends, and was blessed with fantastic professors. I also kept up with my historical trend of working part-time jobs, all while part of my school's law review and being very active in other groups and activities on campus. I even met my now-husband, while running for the Student Bar Association.

My first job out of law school was at a large investment adviser and broker-dealer, which was headquartered in Chicago, Illinois. This position was the start of my career in the world of corporate America, as opposed to the more conventional track of practicing in a law firm. As a nearly lifelong Floridian, accustomed to pristine weather, the uncompromisingly cold Chicago winter was a rude awakening. To this day, I'm still surprised that I survived my first winter in Chicago.

The next work opportunity I pursued was with a Chicago-based compliance consulting firm, where I rapidly accelerated and began working autonomously with private equity funds, real estate funds, hedge funds, and other types of investment advisory firms. It was at this time when, with the permission of my then-boss, I landed a Chief Compliance Officer role for a growing hedge fund, while simultaneously maintaining a few dozen other clients for which I was performing outsourced compliance work. This was a significant accomplishment because although I had the necessary qualifications and was well-suited for the role, I was only a couple of years into my career. Candidly, 27 years old is by no means the average age of a Chief Compliance

Officer. Despite my young age, I exceeded the expectations of my clients and colleagues. I look back on that opportunity fondly and remain close with that firm to this day.

The compliance consulting firm was an unbelievably fast-paced work environment, which I credit for the depth and scope of my knowledge base in the world of securities compliance. With no exaggeration, it would have taken me over a decade to amass the amount of experience and client contact that resulted from working at the firm for just a couple of years. It was a whirlwind of activity, but thankfully I had previously encountered 100-hour workweeks *(albeit in my pre-law school life)*.

Thereafter, I moved to another compliance consulting firm and continued growing the depth of my expertise in securities compliance. I began working with a broader group of clients, both geographically and with regard to the type of financial services firms that I worked with. I promptly identified a scaling issue on the business side of things. Unless a firm is well-equipped with knowledgeable compliance staff, there is a hard limit to the number of new clients that can be onboarded. With limited internal resources and a retainer-based engagement model, a compliance consulting firm cannot be the end-all, be-all for every one of its clients.

It was at this time in my career that I encountered a critical turning point. I was incredibly grateful for the opportunities I had received, but I had accomplished all that I could while working for someone else at a compliance consulting firm. For those of you familiar with securities compliance and financial regulations, please read on, otherwise perhaps skip the following "Been there, done that" list.

- I registered dozens of investment advisers and alternative asset managers with the SEC and other state-specific regulatory authorities.

- I prepared and completed annual and as-needed amendments to Form ADV, Form PF, Form D, Blue Sky, 13F, and 13H filings.

- I reviewed and advised clients on fund offering documents, including private placement memorandums, marketing material, website disclaimers, etc.

- I developed, reviewed, and revised compliance programs, including compliance manuals and accompanying policies and procedures, compliance calendars, anti-money laundering policies, business continuity and disaster recovery policies, cybersecurity policies, and written information security policies.

- I conducted dozens of annual compliance program reviews and mock SEC examinations, as well as assisted with the entire process of SEC and state-securities examinations.

- I collaborated with high-level executives and managed relationships with outside counsel and other service providers.

- I engaged in due-diligence meetings with current and prospective investors, large allocators, and alternative asset managers on behalf of clients.

- I conducted annual compliance training and provided various annual compliance certifications, including employee acknowledgments of the compliance manual and code of ethics, red flags certifications, securities holding reports, vendor security questionnaires, no insider trading certifications, and outside business activities disclosure forms and questionnaires.

You name it. I did it. I worked hard, but I was also afforded unique opportunities that I capitalized on. Although I believe it is very important to have an "attitude of gratitude," it is equally important to stay true to yourself and understand that your professional needs may evolve.

It is worth noting that at this point in my personal life, I was recently engaged to be married and planning for a destination wedding in Naples, Florida. As you might know and/or have experienced, wedding planning is in and of itself a full-time job. I was still working for a consulting firm with retainer-based clients, which was comparable to having a few dozen jobs and bosses. Despite my drive, work ethic, and ability to multi-task, I found myself longing for the comfort and security of an in-house position where I could focus on working for one client. *What a concept.*

Realizing that it was time for a change, I began interviewing for in-house compliance positions, ranging from Compliance Associate to Chief Compliance Officer. Although each interview had its differences, there was one familiar trend. Every interview seemed to be better than the last. I frequently made it through several rounds of interviews for a particular position. However, the result of countless "final interviews" was either, "You are such a great fit, but we think you would be bored here, as you've conducted this work for dozens of clients at a time." or "You are such a great fit and meet every one of the required qualifications, except you don't have 15 years of the post-law school experience."

I suddenly found myself in a peculiar circumstance, where the depth of my experience did not accurately correspond with my years out of law school. I was encountering a professional roadblock solely based on my years of experience, which came as a bit of a shock to my ego. I didn't want to do a disservice to the expertise that I had acquired in securities compliance, by going too far outside of my niche. Try as I might, I just couldn't seem to find that perfect fit with an in-house role.

My then-fiancé, now-husband, aptly suggested that I launch my own compliance consulting firm. Don't get me wrong. I pride myself on my unwavering confidence, but the unsuccessful interviews I was encountering had me questioning myself. Not to mention, I did not become a lawyer with any intention of being my own boss. I kept telling myself that there must be more to learn through working for someone else and that I just wasn't ready to go out on my own.

Although entrepreneurship had never previously occurred to me, after a few meetings with mentors of mine, they also suggested that I should start my own firm. My immediate response to that suggestion was, "You got my wedding invitation, right?" which I then followed with my laundry list of reasons as to why it didn't make sense at this stage of my life and how I never intended to be my own boss.

Unbelievably, I think I may have even put my age as a "con" on my pros vs. cons list when I was trying to determine if that was a feasible next step for my career. Nobody even close to my age had launched a compliance consulting firm of this nature, so who was I to think that I had what it takes. I had countless excuses for how and why it didn't make sense to start my own firm.

Nevertheless, I stepped back to think about how I wanted my career to progress and what I wanted for my future. The idea of creating my own schedule became increasingly appealing. If I was going to work a 100-hour work week, why not have it be for myself and on my own terms. Knowing I wanted to grow my family, I considered how nice it would be to have the flexibility to work from home or even one day create what could turn into a family business.

Taking a leap of faith, I decided to trust in the potential that others saw in me before I could quite see it myself. By no means did I have it all figured out. As with anything, there is no "perfect time," nor is there a clear roadmap to launching your own business. However, sheer grit, determination, and a commitment to excellence paired with the support of your mentors and loved ones, definitely does not hurt. Alas! An Accidental Entrepreneur was born!

During the first year of my firm's launch, I went to every networking event under the sun. I searched for events that utilized any buzzword, even remotely related to my industry. I often attended multiple events or otherwise several one-on-one coffee meetings throughout one particular day. I just could not say no to a good introduction. I quickly met and made meaningful connections with over 1,000 people.

While spending much of the first year of my business clientless, I tried not to doubt myself. There were definitely moments where I thought about the security (not to mention, reliable salary) that I would have been provided if I had continued to pursue a conventional job. Nevertheless, I stayed persistent and devoted myself to working as hard as necessary to bring my plan to fruition. My dedication and investment in myself began to pay off, and through word of mouth, I began onboarding clients. I also discovered different ways to avail myself as a compliance resource, such as through in-house and of counsel positions, as well as through strategic partnerships. When I launched my firm, my intention was, and continues to be, providing quality compliance work and empowering a strong culture of compliance for my clients and within this industry. I am passionate about collaboration and assisting other financial services firms in creating new revenue streams, by developing new service offerings; growing their reputation by engaging a new subject-matter expert in compliance; improving client retention by providing a more comprehensive service offering; or bridging a gap through personnel transitions, special projects, etc. There are plenty of fish (i.e., prospective clients) in this professional sea, and I'm not too proud to help others succeed.

Every day, I continue to grow and learn. Three and a half years later, I look back fondly and with an appreciation for what it took to get where I am today, and I wouldn't change it for the world. When I consider the trajectory of my personal, educational, and professional experiences, I realize that becoming an entrepreneur wasn't an accident at all.

I have been married for three years now, and my husband and I are welcoming our first child into the world. Things couldn't be busier, and I couldn't be more grateful. I am excited to see what is in store for my future. Sometimes I look back and reflect on how far I've come, but now I can't help but think that I'm just getting started.

Samantha Bonamassa

Samantha Bonamassa has focused her career on developing and implementing customized compliance programs for SEC, CFTC, and FINRA regulated financial services organizations. She has worked with over 100 investment advisers, alternative asset managers (private equity funds, hedge funds, real estate funds, venture capital funds, etc.), and broker-dealers, both domestically and internationally, with assets under management ranging from several hundred million to several billion dollars.

Samantha has held roles such as Chief Compliance Officer and Interim Chief Compliance Officer for SEC-registered investment advisory firms, "Of Counsel" for law firms, and has worked for various securities compliance consulting firms.

In 2018, Samantha founded Coast to Coast Compliance. Armed with her unique insight and enthusiasm, she takes the chaos out of compliance and brings a wide range of knowledge regarding corporate and securities compliance matters to immediately and meaningfully impact her clients' businesses, by enhancing or otherwise creating an exceptional and customized compliance program, while cultivating a strong culture of compliance.

Among other offerings, Samantha conducts SEC, ERA, and state registration services, as well as develops compliance programs and annual compliance program reviews. She also performs mock SEC examinations, provides regulatory examination assistance, and offers interim and fractional Chief Compliance Officer services and support, which includes ongoing compliance monitoring, training, and independent testing.

Samantha received her B.A., cum laude, from the University of Florida and her J.D. from the Ave Maria School of Law. She is admitted to the Florida Bar and the Illinois Bar.

Samantha was a panelist at the Venture for Women and Diversity Summit, as well as a presenting speaker at the Schaumburg Business Association and Chicago Bar Association. She has also been a featured speaker on Blog Talk Radio's Chicago's Legal Latte.

Samantha is the Director of Events for Chicago Financial Women and is actively involved in several other networking organizations.

Samantha Bonamassa
Coast to Coast Compliance
Chicago, IL
312-219-2929
Samantha@c2ccompliance.com
www.c2ccompliance.com
www.LinkedIn.com/Company/Coast-to-Coast-Compliance

Customizable Compliance Testing and Review Program

In a constantly evolving regulatory environment, my mission is to enhance or otherwise build an exceptional compliance program for my clients.

Whether you are a newly formed investment adviser and need to implement a compliance testing and review program, or an established firm seeking to improve upon its existing compliance testing and review program, this excel document can be customized for the needs of your firm and its personnel.

This customizable compliance testing and review program can help give your firm and staff the credit it deserves, by providing the framework for maintaining an effective compliance program and cultivating a strong culture of compliance.

www.c2ccompliance.com/free-customizable-compliance-testing-and-review-document

Susan M. Gold

Attracting Your Ideal Client. The Ones That Make You Money and Make You Happy!

Who doesn't want to work with clients who make you money and make you happy? It seems pretty obvious, right? Sure. However, it is easier said than done, although it can be done. There are three secrets that will get you on the right track to do just that.

Secret #1: The WHO

Not all clients are created equal. You need to identify the kind of client that gives you joy, sees the value you offer, and is willing to pay you for it. The key is to get very clear on who makes you money and who makes you happy. The thing is, you instinctively already know which clients make you happy when you work with them. You know who they are because they tend to stand out. They're the ones that make you feel like, "WOW, I get paid to do this? I'm so lucky!" The trick is taking those instinctive feelings and turning them into a replicable approach to growth.

By the way, I didn't feel like this most of my corporate life, including the first eight years of working for myself! That all changed when I created a coaching service that aligned with the people that wanted to pay me for my value and made me happy to get up every day and work with them.

Here's the thing: if you don't do this, you'll lose time and money. You'll get burnt out easily. It's difficult to stay motivated if your clients do not value you. Have you ever decided, well, I'm not going to that networking event because

I don't get any referrals, or I don't even know who to ask to be introduced to? They say 90% of success is just showing up, but you'll see results if you show up in the "right room" to be seen and heard by your ideal clients.

Attracting clients that make you happy AND make you money is the path to success. You'll do your best work, feel fulfilled and make a difference for those clients. That will result in referrals and testimonials. Think about your client list and with whom you've really enjoyed working. Who lights you up and makes you feel good about the work you do? Write their names down. They're the seeds to your success.

I'd like to tell you about a client I worked with — we'll call her Lisa*. She's been working in accounting and bookkeeping for about 20 years. She was considering buying her partner out. We had a conversation about the clients she served. Her basic accounting clients were mostly non-profits, restaurants, and retail, that were struggling through the pandemic. In our coaching sessions, she considered what she loved doing and who she loved working with — and guess what — she didn't love bookkeeping! She really loved the high-level accounting and controller work. It is a role that has a greater impact on the big decisions a company makes. So, we dug further into that.

I asked her which markets she was able to serve in that controller role, and she revealed that she had a specialty and a passion for working with condo associations. It is really complex, and she had a deep understanding of that world. She loved doing it. She thought, "This is the work that I love doing, and these are the people I love to help because they are challenging. I'm really good at it, and it makes me happy." Well, guess what? The company she was considering buying didn't have any of her ideal clients since they were primarily bookkeeping clients!

When she really started getting clear about THE WHO she wanted to work with, it led to all kinds of decisions. The most important one was choosing *not* to buy this business. She realized that she would be miserable if she did. She would be spending time with clients that didn't make her money or make her happy.

This clarity led her to do things differently. She stopped networking in the places she used to and really thought about where she would find the right contacts for condo associations. She soon gained clients because she was really passionate about them, and she knew a lot about this space. This resulted in her making 40% more working for herself vs. working for her previous partner, whom she had considered buying out. Let me repeat this: she's making 40% more revenue and has started her own business with her ideal client targets she absolutely loved. Guess what? All the money was hers! She chose not to buy the company that was going to make her miserable.

Who do you want to work with, and what is your niche? Are you crystal clear on your WHO? That is the key foundationally. Anyone you are working with for your marketing execution (such as your website, brand design, or content) will ask who your target market is. How clear are you on a scale of 1 (not clear) to 10 (very clear) on the WHO you want to work with — the ideal clients that make you money and make you happy? Can you really describe the type of business you want to work with? Are you in that place where you are stuck working with clients that make you decent money, but are draining the life out of you because you are not doing the kind of work you love or getting paid well to do it? Maybe you are working with clients that you can "get" but not making the money you should for the value you are giving your clients?

You really MUST work with clients that make you money and make you happy. If you don't, you're on a slow slide to disappointment and potential failure. To avoid that path, you need to be very clear on WHO you want to work with.

Secret #2: The WHAT

How many times have you read or heard a marketing message from a company that says very little or doesn't grab your attention? Maybe it doesn't speak directly to you or captures you on any emotional level? It could also all just be about THEM and their services. All you hear is "blah, blah, blah...." If you speak to the heart of your ideal client's pain points (their issues, challenges, and struggles), you can connect with them in a powerful way. They hear that you get them, what they are feeling, and what they are dealing with. It creates the desire to hear more from you. They want to know how you impact their issues and the value you have to offer. At this point, that's more important than your process and approach or the variety of services and packages you offer. Most prospects can't take that in all at once. However, if you talk about their issues and perspective, then you have the start of a dialog that can progress to engagement.

Here's an extra secret: many entrepreneurs really struggle with marketing. Most small business owners haven't had any marketing training. However, to be successful in business, you have to learn how to create leads. Messaging is the critical first piece to getting those leads.

Most entrepreneurs focus on what they do vs. how they have an impact on their client's problems. Many spend a lot of time talking about their process on their website, in social media, networking "one minutes," and in feature presentations. As a business owner, you need to generate sales and create leads to feed your business. Learning how to do this is the key to success. Your message is everything — in your networking, on your website, and everywhere you "appear."

When you know who your ideal clients are, then you create a marketing message that focuses on their problems. It's not about you. It's about them. If you don't know their problems, ask them. They will tell you, even if you draw it out of them slowly. Ask them what keeps them up at night and drives them crazy? What issues seem insurmountable? Push them to get to the core issue and help them separate symptoms from causes. Once you do, explain how you can impact those problems. Show how you bring value to them that is different — your secret sauce.

Once you understand how to create messaging, it captures their attention. They will want to hear more from you. This is how we engage. Imagine being in the right room with the right message in front of the right people. That is when the magic happens.

Let me share with you the power of getting your marketing message right. I worked with Rachel*, an operations professional in healthcare and non-profits. She was thinking about starting her own business. Naturally, she thought, "Oh, I'll work with healthcare and non-profits because that's my background and where all my contacts are." Logical, right?

However, as she did the work of identifying the WHO she was meant to serve, we discovered her passion wasn't really with the healthcare and non-profits at all. It was more with helping business services, such as accounting firms. She loved working with professionals that needed her help with business processes. Rachel had a brain for solving process problems. She found that the business services market was underserved.

Rachel now had her WHO. We then focused on the marketing message — an area where she struggled because she was process-focused and naturally wanted to talk about the process first. However, this just wasn't resonating with her prospects. Because of that, she was struggling to get new clients. Once we refocused her message on the results her clients would realize from working with her, everything changed. She learned how to identify the top four process issues that accounting firms had and mapped her marketing message to those problems and the results they needed. Rebecca helped her ideal clients see that she identified with them and understood their problems. This created a stronger connection.

That clarity around the WHO and adjusting her message to focus on problems and results helped her land a large project that turned into a huge client. It grew her business by 200% in just one month, all on the strength of clearly understanding the WHO and having a well-articulated message.

The equally important messages regarding HOW she solved her clients' problems and the results she brought to that specific target market came later. That story, in turn, has created more clients for her — when they hear her pitch, they say, "Yes, I want what she has, and I want her to help me solve these problems!"

Secret #3: The WHERE

If you have the ideal client target that makes you money and makes you happy, and you have the right message, then you need to know WHERE those messages should appear to connect with them. Many entrepreneurs waste time and energy being in the "wrong room."

This means that they are sending their message to everyone except their ideal clients. It could be the wrong type of networking group — it may be too general or just not targeted at your ideal clients. Just because you are posting on social media doesn't mean you are reaching a lot of people, let alone your ideal clients. It is likely that you are just not getting heard by the people that need to hear your message. You know you can make a big impact on their challenges, but they don't know it.

How do you get in the right room? You go to them. Who is your ideal target? Think about your ideal clients. Where do they meet? What associations are they a member of? What networking groups do they go to? What social media groups do they belong to? Are they on social media? If you go where they are, then you can make your case for value.

When I met Tracy*, she was a frustrated and burnt-out professional after spending decades as a mental health therapist. She wanted to work as a relationship coach, something she loved doing. In fact, it was the favorite part of her work. We identified her ideal client as senior executive women. These women were great with their career growth but often had significant relationship issues. Tracy was a member of several local women's networking groups. However, she wasn't attracting the level of career women she desired to work with. She loved the relationships she had developed in her own city and had to let go of the personal attachments and leave the women she had grown to respect. For her, meeting the types of professional women she wanted to work with required her to leap into the national networking arena. Understanding what was possible in networking and joining organizations that attracted the very experienced female corporate executives she was passionate about was a game-changer for her. She became a better gatekeeper for her schedule, was more selective about who she'd take on as a client, and as a result, gained more time to write and publish herself, so she would have the visibility and credibility she needed. Now that she's in the "right room" with her ideal clients, her hourly rate went from $180 to $300. She also gained a significant ROI on her time. She's enjoying Mondays now focused on her writing and networking, bringing in her ideal clients, and making a difference.

The takeaway is that this all happened because she changed her WHERE. By moving to a national audience for networking, speaking, and publishing, she was able to bring great value to her clients and, by doubling her rate, find more time to invest in being in the right room to attract even more ideal clients. She felt in charge of her business, in control of the clients she took on, and she was in the right places to attract the right prospects. Business is booming.

To close, let's review the keys to attracting your ideal clients that make you money and make you happy: first, be crystal clear on WHO your ideal clients are.

Second, craft a "WOW" message that focuses on your ideal client's pain points and the impact you have on them. Deliver a message that causes them, your WHO, to respond and want to have a conversation.

Third, be in the right room to be heard by the right people, so you are WHERE your ideal clients can hear and see you.

On the surface, the process I've described above seems easy — but believe me, it's not! It's challenging to do this work on your own business, and it requires a deep dive into the core of your business or what you want it to be. However, with the right tools and your knowledge of your very best clients, your business can move from faltering to flying in no time.

I want to leave you with one of my favorite quotes from Steve Jobs.

"The only way to do great work is to love what you do."

—Steve Jobs

*Names have been changed.

Susan M. Gold

With decades of strategic marketing, sales, and business experience, Susan specializes in helping business owners be authentic and to leverage their "WHY" while aligning with who they want to work with, what services they want to offer, and to enable them to get paid for their value. She loves the deep connection with her clients, as she experiences their transformation as they work on their marketing strategies. Her mission is simple — to help her clients to find their ideal clients, build genuine connections with their clients and grow revenue in the process.

Surviving 30 years of experience in the corporate world, Susan had no idea that all those years would ultimately lead to becoming an entrepreneur. Her marketing journey started in "the trenches," working as an account executive for several advertising agencies, most notably Rizzo Simons Cohn, rated the #1 New England Ad Agency by Adweek at that time. She continued her corporate marketing career, working as Vice President for several Fortune 500 companies, such as Fidelity Investments, Fleet Financial Group, and a subsidiary of globally ranked Zurich Investments. An MBA graduate from Simmons College in Boston in 2000, Susan climbed the corporate ladder, becoming one of four women in the top 200 executives at Liberty Mutual, a Fortune 100 company. Susan left the corporate world to start her consulting practice, Gold & Partners LLC, in 2010. She recently introduced her marketing strategy coaching business, Susan Gold Coaching, focusing on the small business owner and entrepreneur.

When she's not helping her clients get more clients, Susan explores her artistic and creative passions as an artist, quilter, gardener, tap dancer, and neophyte golfer. She lives on the seacoast in New Hampshire and enjoys the Piscataqua River and the Atlantic Ocean with her husband, children, and grandchildren.

Susan M. Gold
Susan Gold Coaching
Portsmouth, NH
978-771-0848
Susan@SusanGoldCoaching.com
www.SusanGoldCoaching.com

---

4 Must-Do Action Steps to Attract Your Ideal Clients

Promoting and growing your own company is a challenge for all small business owners. It all starts with a strategy. Follow these 4 Action Steps (and there's a bonus tip too!), and you'll be on your way to creating your strategy to attract your most desirable clients.

https://Book.SusanGoldCoaching.com/gift

Sallie C. Wagner

*How to Reclaim Your Power with M*S*G*

"Sallie, he's gone!"

My mother's voice awakened me. I knew that my husband had died.

We had been keeping vigil. The time had come.

There were so many feelings. I didn't know what to feel. So, I felt numb — numbness, punctuated by knee-buckling pain and grief. I also felt guilt. I fell asleep. Maybe if I hadn't fallen asleep, he wouldn't have died.

Backing up from there, days before, he told me how tired he was. I knew what he was telling me. He was too tired to fight anymore. I told him that it was okay. If he needed to go, he could go. He asked if the children would be okay and if I'd be okay. I lied, and I told him yes, we would be okay.

It was now 4 am on Sunday, and he was gone. I knew that I had killed him. If only I hadn't given him permission. If only I hadn't fallen asleep.

Each of us has a story of pain, loss, or change. There are dramatic changes, such as births, deaths, marriages, divorces, job loss/change, and relocations. There are also less dramatic changes. They are no less significant. I call it "life creep" when you wake up one day and wonder what happened with your life.

My husband and I were married for almost 23 years. For 23 years, I had known myself in relation to him. Without him, I didn't know who I was anymore. Truth be told, I didn't know who I was before he died. For too long, quite possibly for my entire life, I had been living somebody else's life. I was a non-player character in my own life. It was as if my life were planned and ruled by outside forces, such as Alien Overlords.

It was all because of Apps: Mind Apps, Paradigms, and Alien Overlords.

You know what apps do to your phones and other devices. They slow things down, drain the battery, and sometimes have competing purposes. Mind Apps do the same thing in our lives. They live in your subconscious mind, which is like your operating system. They're the programming that determines the results you get in your life. That programming competes with itself, and you, for control.

Your Apps likely started out as useful — chunking skills, knowledge, and experience into shortcuts to help you navigate and make sense of the world. It is like apps for walking, talking, and driving. They are all incredibly useful.

However, some of your Apps may actually now work against you and what you consciously want in your life. They work in your subconscious mind to sabotage all the wonderful intentions you hold in your conscious mind.

During times of stress, anxiety, worry, times when we're busy running our lives, careers, businesses, which seems like pretty much all the time, we run on autopilot. We revert to our default settings, which are our manufacturer's settings. Those settings tell us what to think and believe about how the world works. The problem is, the things they tell us aren't always true and accurate. That's the crux of it.

You see, it's not what you don't know that holds you back. It's what you do know, that's not true, that holds you back.

So many times, the solution to our challenges is not to learn more, not to learn what we don't know. The solution is to un-learn what we know that's not true.

What do you know — that's not true — that's holding you back?

Why do we "know" things that are NOT true?

It's because of Apps from families, society, and the world. They tell us things that are not true, and we believe it. We're bombarded with messages that we have to be a certain way, look a certain way, wear certain clothes, own certain cars, to be worthy, and to be loved.

We're told we're too much this, not enough that. All those messages, all that programming holds us back from living the life that makes us come alive. So how do you reboot your thinking, uninstall those Apps, and install new Apps that allow you to make conscious choices?

The first step is to recognize that everything is a choice. It is your choice. When you understand this truth, you can begin the process. Just take the first step and decide.

There I was. My first husband had died. Mercifully, time passed — you've heard the saying that time heals all wounds. Let me tell you, that's absolute crap! Time does not heal all wounds. You can put that in the category of things I know now that I wish I'd known then.

Time doesn't heal. How we use time either heals or doesn't heal. When we're purposeful and intentional about healing, we heal. We can't just wait it out.

It was a big mistake on my part.

Nevertheless, time passed. My children and I pieced our lives back together. My kids grew up, I grew up, and they got married, I got remarried. However, I was still living somebody else's life. I kept asking myself, where did I go wrong? How and when did I get so far off track?

When I was a child, I always wanted to be a teacher. In college, I majored in Theology. I started in physics, ended up in metaphysics, and planned to become a professor of Theology.

Then I met my first husband. The first night we met, he said, you should be a lawyer. Guess what? I'm a lawyer. I spent my career living somebody else's vision for my life. It looked pretty good on paper, but it felt pretty yucky inside. I was out of place in my own skin.

Life events then reconnected me to my earlier vision for my life of being a teacher. This time, I listened to the message that life was sending me. I recalibrated and focused on teaching opportunities. When I did that, everything changed to the point where I had to scale back. Yet, the universe still wasn't done with me — it never is!

Eventually, perhaps a bit reluctantly, I followed the trail of bread crumbs that led me to life coaching. I finally listened again and answered my calling to live the life that makes me come alive!

It's scary to make that decision and that commitment.

As soon as I did, part of me argued for why I couldn't... It wasn't a good time. It wasn't convenient. I was running multiple businesses already. How could I take on even more? Another part of me knew that great opportunities never show up when it's convenient or when it's comfortable. Great things occur on the other side of what's comfortable.

I made the decision to let the part of me that wants to come alive and win over the part that's afraid. It was a long journey, yet I still got there. I got here. I know that there are steps I could have taken that would have accelerated that journey for me. I could have taken the shortcut rather than the scenic route.

Therefore, I've created a protocol to guide you to create and take your own shortcut. It will save you time and effort and, perhaps, mistakes along the way.

It's 3 X 3 — three sets of three things to remember.

Here's the 1st set of three steps to begin the process of defeating the Alien Overlords to reclaim your power over your own life.

Those 3 Steps are M*S*G. Mindset, Skillset, Get Off Your Asset!

Mindset is not just thinking happy thoughts, like Peter Pan. Mindset is having faith. It is not necessarily religious faith, although it may also be that. It is faith that you will prevail. At the same time, you must be courageous enough to confront the facts of your circumstances, and the reality of what's happening in your life.

It all starts with Mindset. However, most of the time, we need to take some steps to get the right Mindset. That's where Skillset comes in.

Skillset includes new skills and new knowledge of how to change your thinking to have the right Mindset. One important skill is goal setting. Three guidelines you can use to set your goals are — make it big, ask the right questions, and be specific.

The first principle is — make it big!

Are your goals big enough?

Those Mind Apps (those things we know that are not true) show up in subtle ways, especially in the goals we choose for ourselves. Be generous with yourself in time, money, and in commitment to your own development. It is crucial to value yourself and affirm your worth.

Set big goals!

The second principle is, ask the right questions. The quality of your life is determined by the quality of the questions you're willing to ask. It is important to ask the hard questions.

You've heard of the seven levels deep approach. Seven levels are just a start. Instead of seven levels, think of the process as an infinite onion. You are continuously peeling off layers, in a never-ending quest to get to the core.

Here's the first layer of the onion. Ask yourself, are you successfully discontent? Like me, does your life look good on paper yet doesn't feel so good on the inside? Doesn't it feel as good as you thought it would or should? We hide in the questions we don't ask. We allow others to hide in the questions we don't ask. There's no hiding here.

You must keep asking questions.

The last point for goal setting is, be as specific as possible in stating your goals. If you don't specify, the universe will fill in the blanks. You may not get the results you intend. Remember, words matter. We've all heard about the guy who wishes for a million bucks, and suddenly he's surrounded by deer. Don't be like that guy.

Okay, we've talked about Mindset and Skillset. It's now time to get off your Asset!

Once you identify your goals, you're ready to take action. However, be prepared… what comes next is what stops most people before they get started. As they start to manifest a new Mindset, they get stopped by fear. Fear shows up as indecision, distraction, and self-sabotage. Fear is a Mind App, which, as you know, means it can be subtle. It doesn't announce that it's here to keep you from getting the results you want in life.

It sounds like the voice of reason. It says things like…

- How am I going to do that?

- I've never done that before.

- Now's not a good time.

- Should I really be doing this?

- I can't do that.

Have you heard those voices, or others?

Don't be the person who is pushed by fear. Allow yourself to be pulled by the vision of the life you're creating for yourself! It comes down to fear or faith. You make the choice. It's all about deciding and making a commitment to and for yourself. It's that decision and start, which stops most people. So, decide and take action! It is important to use and not just sit on your assets.

That's the first set of 3 — M*S*G.

The second set of three — three steps you can take to start moving in the right direction. Now that you've decided on your goals, you're ready to take action by creating a system to move you toward your goals.

The first step, write your goals down, will increase your chances of success to 56%.

The second step is to share your goals with somebody. It can be family, friends, or a goal buddy.

Why don't we share our goals? Isn't it because we're afraid to fail? Have you ever failed? Has anybody not failed? Failure is part of the system. It's a tool, not an outcome. It's a resource that you manage, just like all the other resources in your life. When you manage it properly and make it part of your system, you'll find your success. Take the risk, and share your goals. When you share your goals and then identify action steps to take toward your goals, you increase your chances of success to 64%.

Those action steps (including the system and structure) are crucial. This is because goals alone won't get you there. Without action steps, your goals are just nice pictures on that vision board you made. Instead of focusing exclusively on your goals, create a reliable system. It must be something that you can easily, readily, willingly, and happily repeat every day. That's goal-setting to the present. Then, you succeed every day, not by reaching the goal but by moving in the right direction.

You're already 64% of the way there!

The third step in your system (when you make weekly progress reports to your goal buddy) is the accountability factor. It will help you to increase your chances of success to 76%.

That's our second set of 3.

You have the framework and the infrastructure you can use to build your own unique system to get the results you want to see in your life.

All it takes is 100% commitment. Anything less than 100%, even 99.999%, is so hard! It is filled with excuses, and reasons, not to take the steps that will lead to our goals. 100% commitment is so easy! There are no excuses or reasons, just doing. You simply need to follow your system every day. Every day, you should move in the direction of your goals.

It always comes down to reasons or results. You make the choice.

I invite and challenge you. Commit yourself 100%.

You start with M*S*G.

Mindset — Change your Mindset to one of success.

Skillset — Learn and practice the skills that will move you forward in your success.

Get Off Your Asset, by taking action to bring that success into the landscape of your reality.

You have to take action to achieve your goals.

The right Mindset and Skillset will empower you to take the right action and make that 100% commitment — to you!

So, where are you with your M*S*G? Is it (are you) powerful enough to take on the Alien Overlords? When you answer, "YES!"… you're ready for your last set of 3 — my 21-day challenge.

First, for 21 days, maintain the Mindset to get the results you want in life.

Second, for 21 days, develop the Skillset to attain and maintain the right Mindset.

Third, for 21 days, take action, by developing a system to move you in the direction of your goals — every day.

Report back to your accountability partner each week and share your results. Report on the Mindset that you attained and maintained and the Skillset that you acquired and honed. Report on the system that you developed and repeat every day. You can then trust that you will begin to get the results you want to see in your life!

Remember, as Ralph Waldo Emerson said, "The only person you are destined to become is the person you decide to be."

Decide for you.

Make that commitment to you.

Reclaim your power with M*S*G!

Sallie C. Wagner

Sallie C. Wagner is a speaker, author, lawyer, real estate broker and instructor, and life coach.

Your What's Next Strategist and Life Alchemist, Sallie incorporates outcome-based techniques, such as EFT (Emotional Freedom Techniques), Evolved NLP (Neurolinguistic Programming), and trauma-aware modalities, to help you get concrete results, as you ditch those unwanted behaviors and habits, fears, and phobias, limiting beliefs and decisions, that keep you from living your best life.

Sallie's signature coaching program is REBOOT Your Thinking: How to Install and Uninstall Mind Apps. This comprehensive program guides you to achieve life-altering, mind-bending results as you identify and get rid of Mind Apps (paradigms), so you can move forward with your life the way you really want to be living it!

Sallie's continuing mission is to impact lives, as she coaches and guides you to get rid of behaviors, beliefs, and decisions that hold you back, so you can fully embrace and integrate the challenges that life brings in order to discover, create, and live the life that makes you come alive!

Sallie spent the majority of her law career in the corporate world, in various industries. In addition to her other initiatives, she currently provides broker and contract compliance services to real estate brokerages throughout Florida. Sallie provides timely assistance to agents on contract questions and transaction pitfalls.

Sallie also owns and operates a real estate school, providing exceptional educational opportunities for real estate professionals throughout Florida. Classes are available for those seeking a license, as well as those who have a license and are seeking post-license and continuing education courses.

A native of North Carolina and long-time resident of Kansas City (Missouri), Sallie finally found the ruby slippers. She currently has headquarters in the Tampa Bay area, Florida, USA.

Sallie C. Wagner
Intentional Life Coaching, LLC
Parrish, FL
816-616-5403
SWagner@SallieWagnerEnterprises.com
SallieWagner.com

M*S*G Mini Coaching Bundle

Are you ready to live the life that makes you come alive?

Claim your complimentary one-month trial membership in the Sallie Wagner Coaching Community on Locals and get access to my M*S*G Mini Coaching Bundle. Discover your unique Mindset, Skillset, and Get Off Your Asset with this 3-part video series, and get concrete actions steps to enhance your M*S*G. You'll strengthen your Mindset for results. You'll build your Skillset of goal setting. You'll find your motivation to Get Off Your Asset and take action with your own systems for success!

Mindset. Skillset. Get Off Your Asset.

When would NOW be a good time to start?

https://SallieWagnerCoaching.Locals.com/support/promo/MSG100

Dawn Marie Gaden

Cancer Cured My Mindset

I believe we are all one thought away from inspired action and the life of our dreams. An inspired action is what it takes to share my story. Taking action was my thing! It's my programming, and I was good at it! Take action, save the day! My husband and I found ourselves with not three kids, but four kids (the last two are twins), in our big, new beautiful home in the woods, where we would raise our boys. It was the perfect American dream family. Then my husband lost his job, and my beautiful life was flipped upside down. Within a matter of months, we went from two toddlers to four kids, house in the woods, and job loss.

So off I went to save the day! I got the job. Funny enough, it was in the county jail. No longer sunny days spent playing in the backyard with boys belly down in the grass searching for bugs. Now I find myself surrounded by windowless brick walls, metal doors slamming shut, cameras on every corner. I was fueling myself with coffee and self-loathing. I was no longer inspiring others to live their best lives — now mocked for trying to "save the hopeless."

I was surrounded by my own prison of anger, self-doubt, resentment, and blame. My body was failing me as it was fueled by toxic thoughts and emotions. I felt useless, ready to escape my life.

"God, give me something else, this, I cannot handle."

So there I stood one day, waiting for God to save me from this prison. To deliver the present that brings me back to my presence. As I stood on the front porch, the phone rang with desperation in my husband's eyes and a pit in my stomach. The doctor's voice said, "It's Cancer."

My next conversation with God was a bit different. "Really!?!?!!? You think I can handle cancer!? What on earth!?!? Are you kidding me? I have boys who need me!" This conversation went on for a while. Until I remembered what I already knew, "Make a choice, Dawn. Are you ready to see the possibility in this, or will you continue to feed the guilt, resentment, and blame?" It was up to me, just one thought away from creating my life, shifting from impossible to possible.

"This obstacle became my opportunity to see my truth."

I chose to leave the job, heal my life, and enjoy my kids. It was the first time since I was 16 that I didn't work! I took two years off to make decisions about cancer treatment, rest, and find joy again. I began working from home, building my business, and making time for my family and play. Family trips to beaches across the country and backyard playtime again. I have created my own business, traveling, speaking, and coaching others to shift their image, take off the superhero cape and live a life of love and joy. It is up to each and every one of us to take full responsibility for our lives.

Neuroscientists say that 95% of what we think, feel, and do comes from the subconscious mind. Take a moment and feel the impact of that! We are living on autopilot, sleepwalking through our lives, creating what we don't want over and over each day.

I made the decision that day on my porch to no longer let old stories, beliefs, or ideas dictate my life and muffle my voice. Do you ever feel like someone else is pulling your strings, that you're not really living your truth, and someone else is in charge?

Erin Now Interrupts the Old Voice and Replaces It

Erin found herself living that kind of life. She found herself living in a manipulative marriage. She was overweight, unhappy, and blamed her husband for her feelings. To top it off, she was fired from her job without notice. In the six months that we worked together, she was willing to see and understand what she had come to believe — that manipulation equals love. If you can get someone to do what you want, no matter what, then you are loved. I helped her let go of that old story and step into happiness, confidence, and self-worth. She chose to believe in herself and shift into a new story of who she wanted to be. She was now aware of choosing the thoughts that fed her feelings, became the master of her mindset, and began loving herself first. Erin began making healthy choices, walking daily, journaling what I call "dump the junk" journaling, then writing her new powerful positive story. She discovered a career that brought her satisfaction, independence, and fulfillment. She became consciously aware of the old voice, when it peeks its nasty head and wants to play the role of manipulation. She is now able to interrupt the old voice and replace it, shifting her self-image from lack, limitation, and poor me, into the confident, healthy, loving woman that she is now.

Wake up to the power within you! Where are you on autopilot, sleepwalking through life, creating what you don't want?

Secrets Into Action

Knowing that I can step out of the chaos in my mind and see choices to create my own story, led me to work with others in the same way.

The secrets to my image shift that I live by and teach my clients are: master your mindset, embody emotions, and create healthy relationships. To put these secrets into action, you must be ready, willing, and able to choose the life you were meant to live and know that you are meant for great things! You have a choice, and you have your own voice that will lead you out of the darkness. It just takes a shift from who you are, to who you want to be. Let go of the old paradigms, which are the stories that you learned along the way that no longer serve you. Step into your greatness and into your truth!

With over two decades in the mindset business, I've had the opportunity to speak to over 10,000 people worldwide and teach the importance of a positive self-image. One of my favorite quotes from my mentor, Wayne Dyer, "Don't die with your music still in you."

Sally Now Marches to the Beat of Her Own Drum

Sally poured her heart and soul into her kids and marriage. She was the All-star stay-at-home mom, who put herself last, and sacrificed herself. She was now divorced, with her kids grown, and moved out. She had no idea who she was. She felt she did everything right. What went wrong? As we worked together to uncover the old story of being a child of an alcoholic, living an unpredictable home life, and decisions fueled by fear, Sally discovered she was living in the story of "what about me, unworthiness, and lack." As she chose to be courageous and strong, she uncovered what she no longer wanted in her life. She cut the strings of autopilot and began discovering her passion, purpose, and joy for living. As we worked together, I helped guide her to realize the lifelong dream of owning her own business. I helped her to step into the image of the confident, happy, and successful business owner, as she opened her own fitness studio during a pandemic, no less! Her life continues to show her where to grow, see possibility and shift her image to embrace her power! She now sets healthy boundaries with others, has a kind, compassionate and respectful relationship, and knows how to interrupt and replace the negative stories. She knows she is worthy of all good. She now marches to the beat of her own drum, letting her music play loud and proud, and also being a phenomenal role model to her kids that you are the keeper of your health, wealth, happiness, and abundance.

What emotion feeds your self-image and needs a shift?

You Are Not Every Thought That You Think

Choosing your thoughts gives you the ability to live your life free from being controlled by your thoughts. Remember that you are not every thought that you think. I ask that you step into your truth and be present with your higher self, your higher mind. That place allows you to see and separate yourself from negative thoughts and then choose the thoughts you want to experience.

Intentionally choose thoughts that empower you to be your very best. Do not let any thought pass by without your awareness. You are not defined by every thought you think or every feeling that you feel. For example, you have the ability, the right, and the obligation to question, "What would life look like if you weren't depressed?" Just because your mom was depressed, or your dad was depressed, or there's a family history of depression, what if it was possible for you not to think negative thoughts? What if it was possible for you to wake up and choose something joyful to see in the day? Look for what's possible. You will find it!

What happens next, you may ask? You've made the decision to choose powerful, positive, and inspired thoughts, then what? What do you do with the thoughts? Have you heard the statement "Thoughts become things?" Well, we have the ability to activate our energy and elevate our state by bringing thoughts, emotions, and movements into action.

Tina Now Gives Herself Permission to Say YES

Tina spent many years in unfulfilled, even toxic and codependent relationships. She changed her hair, clothes, and looks to satisfy whomever she was with. She did not understand why she was unhappy or why the relationships could not be sustained. Recalling her need to please others, stemmed from her childhood experiences. Dad's absence and disappointing no-shows left Tina feeling alone and abandoned, wondering what she did wrong. She believed that she was responsible for her dad's behavior in some way or a cause of it. She was a single mom, a high career achiever, and consistently worked diligently to please others. As a cancer thriver, she also questioned whether or not her stifled self-expression and lack of authentic living was contributing to her body's disease.

Ready, willing, and able to take action, Tina found our practice of movement in our sessions with the intenSati Method, which helped her connect more deeply with her emotions and how her body was feeling. Being able to release emotions that made her feel sick, depressed, or anxious by using high-energy movements and affirmations created the quantum leap she was looking for to create change in her life and relationships. We used a chopping practice where we vigorously chopped our hands in front of the heart to break energetic connections with negative emotions — chopping away self-doubt, unworthiness, anxiety, uncertainty, fear, and lack. She now has the insight and mental muscle to notice emotions without letting them take over her entire body. She is able to use our movement practices with powerful positive self-talk to move the emotions and create clarity in her thoughts, feelings, and actions. She is loving her life and creating loving, healthy relationships — first with herself and then others. She has the confidence to make decisions that are right for her, and to speak her voice, even when others disagree.

She now understands that she can't pour from an empty cup and that filling herself up first is good self-care, not selfishness. Tina continues to say no to what no longer fits in her life, such as dates, just because it's "someone to spend time with." She now gives herself permission to say YES to her bubble baths, long walks, trips, and whatever feeds her soul and defines her new self-image. She is also one of the top salespersons on her team, loves her success, and enjoys mentoring her co-workers.

Our thoughts open the doors to possibility. What do you see as possible for you to live a life you love?

When you connect emotionally with your body, you choose how to show up in all that you do. Remember, you are one choice away from your powerful positive self-image. If you believe you are successful, you are. If you believe you are worthy, you are. If you believe in solvable problems, you will find the answers. With inspired action, you create the Image Shift.

Evan Is No Longer Second-Guessing His Decisions and Being Guided by Fear

Evan was about to lose his six-figure career. He was unable to complete projects. He suffered from anxiety, daily panic attacks, and debilitating stress from a toxic marriage and pending divorce. Trying to hold it together for his kids, personal life, and work, he needed support and tools that he hadn't tried before.

Evan was able to find the shift he needed to begin feeling confident, clear-headed, and worthy using meditation and mindful practices. He increased productivity at work, achieved clearer thinking, and worked with higher confidence. He was able to calm the chaos in his mind and focused more on making important decisions at work, completing projects, and again finding more value and connection with colleagues.

In spite of the pending divorce, Evan felt confident to make the best decisions he could for his kids and personal life. There was no more second-guessing his decisions and being guided by fear. He is now guided by his truth to live an empowered life.

Take 3 minutes every day to breathe, be present, and be grateful for who you are and what you have.

Ready to Step into Action

The shift happens when we're ready to step into action. Evan and many others discovered the third secret to manifesting the life of their dreams: cultivating healthy relationships. It's important to create your power team. We cannot do this work alone. Your community and your tribe will lift you up when you fall, hold you accountable when you try to take shortcuts, and challenge you when you are about to throw in the towel.

The cure for my toxic mindset was not one to be expected. Cancer is usually the poison that so many of us want to rid ourselves of and fear so deeply. For me, it was what woke me up to my power and truth, to become the master of my mind. I consciously chose to create a life I love, a life worth living, and a life full of joy, abundance, and health.

Being someone who likes to do things independently (a bit of a loner, one might say), it took courage to find a team to support me with love, compassion, and understanding. I knew that to grow, heal, and cure my mindset. I had to surround myself with people who would lift me up and help me heal.

That decision took me all the way to New York City from Michigan to become immersed in the intenSati community, where I would learn the practice that healed my mind, body, and my spirit and allowed me to share this practice with many others who are also looking to cure their mindset. There is no destination. This is the journey. This is the adventure of life! Daily inspired action keeps me connected to my team, tuned into my mind, embodying my emotions, and allows me to live my life as I choose.

My favorite quote is by Deepak Chopra. He says, "Every cell in your body is eavesdropping on every thought you think." May this thought be a guiding light for you, as it is for me.

Dawn Marie Gaden

Dawn Marie Gaden is the CEO of Mind Body Counseling and Coaching, an international speaker, and a successful entrepreneur.

Dawn is a powerhouse in the field of personal development. She is internationally known for igniting positive change.

Her global coaching program — The Image Shift, Three Secrets to Manifesting the Life of Your Dreams is powerfully transforming professional women's lives around the world.

Dawn has devoted her life to studying with the best in the field of change work. Dawn has been mentored by speaking icons, like Bob Proctor and Wayne Dyer, and has spoken on stages and podcasts to over 10,000 people.

Dawn is a licensed counselor, coach, registered yoga teacher, and has unique expertise in changing the brain with exercise in a practice called intenSati.

As an intenSati leader, Dawn teaches her clients a whole-body experience that creates a sustainable and powerful image shift that forever impacts their lives.

Dawn was born and raised in Michigan, where she currently lives with her husband Mike of 22 years. She is raising four amazing boys that includes 15-year-old twins! Dawn especially loves paddleboarding, taking long walks on the beach, and going on wild adventures across the country with her family each year.

However, she is most grateful for the gifts she has discovered through her journey with cancer. In this experience, Dawn learned to thrive by living from a heart-centered place, choosing to never compromise her joy and happiness for struggle and limitations.

Dawn Marie Gaden
Mind Body Counseling and Coaching PLLC
Brighton, MI
810-623-7375
Dawn@CreateConsciousLiving.com
www.CreateConsciousLiving.com

Warrior of Love Moving Meditation Audio

Move your body with these powerful positive words to elevate your state and activate positive emotion. Three minutes of creating a positive state every day can change your entire day and set you up for success in all that you do. Change your thoughts, change your state!

https://CreateConsciousLiving.com/landing/warrior-of-love-moving-meditation

Professor Joaquin Jackson
The Desire, The Discipline,
and The Demonstration

It started in my youth, between the ages of 11 and 13, when our local mailman, a Vietnam War army veteran named Mr. Williams, would occasionally stop by our family's business, "Tommy's Barber Shop," which was operated by both of my parents. On those days after Mr. Willams had completed his route, he would teach me martial arts in the shop's backroom. That training assisted in shifting my focus and energy during such a gray period in my life. I'm now thinking, was that the beginning or the end of the beginning? I would continue to practice those moves, until I enlisted into the United States Marine Corps at 19. While in boot camp during the hand-to-hand combat training sessions, I assisted the instructors.

After graduating from boot camp, I received my first duty orders. I was going to be a long way from home and family. Those papers had me stationed in Subic Bay in the Philippines for 15 months. This is where I was taught judo on base by the Marine Corps Base Commander, who was a major. He was a tough devil dog 100%. I was then introduced to boxing by a retired navy veteran and boxing champion, Coach Johnson. I made the boxing team there in Subic Bay, with a record of 4-0. When I was stationed in Okinawa, Japan, I made the Marine Corps boxing team. I was also on the team in Korea. I exchanged martial art techniques with the Korean Rock Marines during guard duty. Even now, I believe that I need and want to be the *complete weapon*. The desire is much stronger now than 20 years ago. I'm still practicing the physical portions of martial arts. However, I would rather use different types of weapons to de-escalate situations. I want to be able to protect myself, those I love, and those who cannot defend themselves.

During my tour, I would look forward to mail calls wherever I was in the world. I noticed when I would receive bulky letters from my Dad. Those letters were filled with the job listings from back home. He would circle a few of the job requirements, all of which required college degrees. Immediately after my tour in the Marine Corps, I took my father's, the Rev. Alonzo Jackson's advice.

I enrolled at Chicago State University, majoring in criminal justice and psychology. I was also enrolled in the ROTC (Reserve Officer Training Corp) advance program. This was my opportunity to transition from a soldier to an officer. *I was determined.* I stayed focused and worked a full-time job every semester. Many things were hanging in the balance.

One Saturday afternoon, I was on campus working on improving my run time. I was just a few seconds off in my two-mile time of 12:17 seconds. This was when there was a major change of events. After my run, I entered the athletic building, turned the corner, and headed to the locker room. I started to notice some unfamiliar sounds coming from the wrestling room. As I stood there at the entrance of the wrestling room door, watching, I witnessed the power of physics being poetically demonstrated in beautiful motion. I was not even sure what I was observing. However, time was of the essence. I needed to clean myself up and get to work on time. As I was preparing to go to work, one of the people from the wrestling room entered the locker room. I started to ask him questions. What were they doing? What was their style? Who was the founder? When was the next class? During the conversation, I realized that I was speaking to the instructor. He was my future teacher, the late Garrett Hawkins, 4th Degree Black Belt in Aikido. I showed up on Tuesday and continued being directly taught by him for eight years, before he made his transition.

Today, I just realized that all of a sudden, I had actually not only just turned the corner in the building. Instead, I had turned the corner of my life into a major experience that has and is having a profound effect on my life and lifestyle and has expanded my consciousness and spirit. I am still learning and teaching Aikido. However, it has created an amazing domino effect in my life. The treasure hunt of this journey has taken over 32 years. It has been documented and is still counting. It started with beginning Aikido until now. I keep recycling the thoughts of this amazing journey. Every type of training has provided me with many experiences that have filled me with gratitude and appreciation for this gift.

The only evidence that I was able to come across were scattered fingerprints of this journey that may have appeared to be hidden but were rather profound and developed stages of Faith in God.

I believe that martial arts must be taught in relation to teaching the wholeness of mankind. This can have a direct result in maximizing their potential. It can awaken and align these three innate ingredients into oneness. The chief instructor must constantly sprinkle these ingredients into the training drills and curriculum. Who are these three generals? They are *mind, body, and spirit.* During the course of my martial arts journey, the wisdom that I have gained is *priceless.* Those generals have shifted in their orders over the decades. This is how they are now aligned in my life, which has led me to understand the last, which was the spirit. Spirit has now become first, and the mind becomes second — strongly finishing with the body being last.

Martial arts has much more to offer than breaking, sweeping, joint locking throwing, and, most of all, tournaments. Having those abilities in your toolbox is indeed important. The caveat of martial arts should be the transformation out of ego and destruction. However, the journey is noticeably aligned with love, peace, and harmony. This transformation is achieved by releasing or awakening new heightened experiences and demonstrations in your life.

The training takes on a different mindset, when the ego is eliminated from the equation. Me vs. everybody is not the reason behind the training. Therefore, training becomes elevated beyond the physical. The connection between fluidity, strength, insight, and creativity makes the journey incredibly transforming.

When you become awake to some experiences that have occurred in your past, you will discover treasures in those experiences. Those golden nuggets hold a lot of weight. It has impacted your life, regardless of the severity of the pain that is linked to those experiences encoded into your emotional memory. The road map of your journey has stored files and videos in your mind that were necessary to bring you to this moment in time. They are evidence that can indicate how you were being protected, taught, guided, and prepared to handle your next experiences.

The real benefits of studying martial arts are beyond what's advertised. The advertisement today should read, "Learn to defeat the enemy within you." Everything else will follow.

My late Aikido Instructor Garrett Hawkins Sensei once shared these philosophical words with me, *"When the student is ready, the teacher would appear."* That statement has haunted me. After his transition, I had been looking for an answer, since we created the largest African American Dojo in the city and state. This scripture comes to mind in 2 Timothy 2:15 KJV "Study to shew thyself approved unto God, a workman that needeth not to be ashamed, rightly dividing the word of truth." I found strength in understanding the quote "When the student is ready." It became evident that prayer, fasting, and meditation produced amazing results. The wisdom in the Book of Proverbs 3:5-6, "Trust in the Lord with all thine heart; and lean not unto thine own understanding. In all thy ways acknowledge him, and he shall direct thy paths."

These were the rocks that I relied upon for 17 years, while running the dojo. I found and understood the call of leadership. The answer was in Ephesians 6:11, "Put on the whole armour of God, that ye may be able to stand against the wiles of the devil."

The answer that I was seeking was spelled out this way. It just made so much sense to me. Allow me to present to you this way.

Take the movie *"The Wizard of Oz,"* for instance. That movie had many gems of life lessons to learn from. The movie's signature statement that was being echoed throughout the movie repeatedly was, "Follow the Yellow Brick Road." They followed it to the end. When the main characters reached their destination, they became instantly dismayed. They were just standing there consciously confused and emotionally bankrupted. They were drastically attempting to re-frame their reality. This dilemma introduced them to self-discovery.

These characters' beliefs reflected that they were controlled by outside factors, rulings, and the government, which shaped their futures. The silver screen showed us the limitations that fear and ignorance produced by an external incident can be caused by an internal urge for change.

They all took a risk to follow the Yellow Brick Road.

Does any of this ring a bell?

You might see where I'm headed!

Follow the Yellow Brick Road! This has been deeply infused into the American culture ego. This blueprint has programmed 99% of Americans. The results will reflect their success when measuring what society has told them how they should look, think, talk, eat, live and dress. This has caused an inside job to destroy themselves. That is why 1% decided to get off the Yellow Brick Road. The real you is in protective custody.

The two or three days of physical training have to be broadened beyond belt chasing. It has to go beyond the dojo (training hall) scope but, more importantly, into a blended society.

How is this possible? I am glad that you asked.

What is self-defense? The answer is straightforward and in plain sight.

"It is defense of one's person or interests against anything or anyone through the use of physical force." The keyword is self before the word defense.

Every major corporation has a defense as an intriguing part of their daily operation. You must activate your defense from the moment that your eyes open in the morning, until you close them at night.

You must guard the divine ideas and dreams you receive. It would be best to reinforce daily what you are watching, speaking, thinking, and your behavior. In the Gospel of John chapter 10:10, "The thief cometh not, but for to steal, and to kill, and to destroy."

You have to keep your vibration high spiritually, mentally, and physically. It is also important to stay prepared to defeat the intentions of what society, family members, friends, associates, data, and statistics deemed you should qualify for.

You have to keep defending why you decided to get off the Yellow Brick Road. This applies even when the profits some days are below your projections. When people quit in the middle of major projects, if you didn't think you were a good candidate for studying martial arts, think again.

You have to learn how to defend on many different levels. This includes who you are listening to and who you want to be directed and guided by. They would be your sensei (teacher) And those that would gather to bring your Divine Idea into a tangible experience. They would be the students. Collectively bringing great minds of like consciousness together is the dojo (the training hall or place of enlightenment). We all have the innate ability to defend ourselves.

When people are confronted with situations that threaten their well-being and safety, they learn something about themselves to either stand their ground or flee because of fear. Whatever the outcome produces is going to warrant future responses with similar or erratic behavior.

It took over 40 years to understand why I was drawn to being a warrior. I trained diligently with those who taught substance and effectiveness. It has been four decades, and the student was now ready again. It was the revelation behind wanting to know how to protect family and friends. I was deeply wounded by that grey area early in my life. That pain consumed my childhood, then spilled over into my adult life.

All of these decades seeking answers to be free had still not happened. My student invited me to attend an upcoming spiritual retreat in several weeks on a Saturday after class. I had no idea what to expect. I didn't expect to be set free from the self-imposed death roll sentence that I had hidden to protect me for 40 years. I didn't know how to be released or disconnect from it. I had become unconscious and comfortable in pain. I had the exact same feeling every time it surfaced. I didn't know how or attempt to get over it. I accepted it because I didn't know what the other side entailed.

The student was ready to get off the yellow brick road. I attended the journey. I met with the facilitator, gave my intentions, and waited. Then I received the sacred medicine. That changed everything forever. What I couldn't overcome in 40 years with the same mindset that kept me imprisoned, was being dismantled within 5-7 hours in an altered mindset while still conscious. I had a conversation with my sister, who passed away from breast cancer at 13 years of age. We were only a year and a half apart. She told me it was time to release her and myself from that pain. She said she was fine, and it was okay. I just lay there weeping, healed, and released from the past. It was later shared that I got involved in martial arts and healing arts because I didn't understand my sister's death at a young age. There was nothing I could do for her. I never wanted to be put in that situation again. At the end of the journey, I discovered a new me. I am free.

In the Book of Ephesians chapter 6:11, "Put on the whole armour of God, that ye may be able to stand against the wiles of the devil." Your gifts and talents are unique fabric pieces that have to be woven into progressively moving mankind forward. You have to be brave enough to consciously get off the Yellow Brick Road and re-navigate.

There are numerous stories in witnessing students come in as beginners, then train, meditate, and awaken their geniuses. One of the students were in the top three state-wide in track and field and in the top 1% of academics when graduated from all academia.

Professor Joaquin Jackson

Joaquin Jackson is a speaker, author, entrepreneur, United States Marine Corps veteran, and self-defense expert. He instructs people on how to protect themselves and their loved ones by getting to safety and home. Professor Jackson has studied martial arts since he was 12 years old, Aikido for 32 years, and Jujitsu for 27 years. He enjoys teaching. However, most of all, he enjoys seeing new students continuously have breakthroughs on the personal, professional, and spiritual levels. He has been taught and trained by a strong cadre of instructors, whom you can google or find on YouTube. He has personally trained thousands of adults and children.

- Motto: All You Need, You Already Have Within You
- Offering: Classes in Self-Defense for Children and Adults

- Why People Should Want to Take Classes with Him: He demonstrates to the students how to build confidence in themselves in an environment that fosters growth through meditation, physical training, and safety techniques.

Professor Joaquin Jackson

Chief Instructor of BMA/Beverly Martial Arts

Illinois

773-750-1564

ProfessorJayJacksonSelfDefense@gmail.com

---

5 Targets to Strike For Self-Defense

"It's best to know how to defend yourself and never use it.
Then to not know and can't defend yourself."

The U.S. Department of Justice states that over the past 20 years, violence and sexual assault toward women have increased dramatically. An estimated 1.9 million women and 3.2 million men are physically assaulted annually in the United States.

You will be provided instructions on how NOT to be a victim and will receive a blueprint for the "Rules of Engagement." The most important factor is "Mind Set," which sets the stage.

Contact Professor Jackson for a FREE in-person or virtual class in Self-Defense and Self-Discovery!

Please, leave your name and email at:

ProfessorJayJacksonSelfDefense@gmail.com or 773-750-1564

Rosie Zilinskas

Discover How to Unlock the Leader Within

I saw him in my apartment building parking lot. He immediately drew me in. He was well-dressed, tanned, and good-looking. I summoned the daredevil within and decided to ask him out. The best idea I had was to write a note and leave it on his Honda CRX windshield. The message went something like this, "Dear Honda CRX guy... My name is Rosie, and I live in apartment 326. Would you like to have ice cream with me?" I included my number and placed the note on his windshield. I drove off to visit my parents, when panic overcame me. "What am I doing? He is going to think I'm nuts!" I turned around, intending to retrieve the note. When I realized that both the car and message were gone, I was mortified. However, things turned around the next day, when he called me. We arranged our first date. I fell head over heels in love because he was so charming. I married an amazing and passionate man with an incredible temper.

I found myself in a terrible situation dealing with his bad temper. When he got angry, his method of operating was to throw and break things. He always excused his anger, by telling me that all men get angry. I was sad, confused, scared, and could not believe that this was my life.

Unfortunately, things only got worse and worse, after we had our two kids. I remember one beautiful fall Sunday morning. The sun was shining, the colors of the tree leaves were gorgeous, and there was a crispness in the air. I woke up, and I was instantly relieved that he had already gone to work at his part-time job. I walked into the kitchen for my morning coffee, and I froze. Right there, in the middle of the kitchen table, was a bullet standing straight up. The scariest part is that my first thought was, "Oh my God, he's going to kill me."

At that moment, I realized that I had the power to change my situation. I grabbed my two little kids, three and six, and the clothes on our back. I ran to my sister's house, where I knew I would be safe. My nerves were shot. Once I calmed down, I asked him to come to hang out at my sister's house after work. He had no idea what I was experiencing.

Ding Dong! He walked in and immediately saw that something was off because my family was surrounding me. That was an intimidating sight, since my dad, brother, and three brothers-in-law were all present.

YOU COULD CUT THE TENSION WITH A KNIFE!!!

I said to him: "I am tired of being afraid and walking on eggshells in my own home. I am leaving you, and I want a divorce."

As expected, he went into a fit of rage. He yelled and screamed all kinds of things. He demanded that I hand over our two kids, which was never going to happen. He stormed out with a drink in his hand, which he threw at my sister's car. He peeled out of the driveway and down the street.

That Is the Moment I Knew I Was Making the Right Choice

Two days later, I was sitting in front of a divorce attorney. He told me that I was a classic example of a domestic violence abuse victim. This moment is imprinted in my brain. The attorney was talking to me, like he was talking about a game of golf instead of my life. I kept thinking, "How is this possible? I am a working professional!" I walked out of that attorney's office in shock and disbelief that this was my life.

The following four years of my life were a living hell. I will admit this was a time of pure fear for me. The fear came from the possibility of losing my kids. My ex-husband alleged that I was an absentee mother. I was angry at his ridiculous claim. I was the one working full-time to support my family, which is what he considered absent. He was a stay-at-home dad and worked part-time. He fought me for full custody of our kids. I was always willing to share parenting and do the right thing for my kids. However, he was not in that mindset. I wasted precious time in dozens of court hearings that did not produce any results. I read useless petitions hoping for a positive outcome, which did not materialize. I even had to hire an attorney that represented my kids called a Guardian ad Litem. I was still working, and it took all the energy within to make it through the workday. I was doing my required work, but I was not going above and beyond. During the day, I worked to keep my job. During the evenings and weekends, I worked to keep my kids.

The sad truth is that intimate partners abuse one in four women and one in nine men in the US.[1] Careers suffer for those who experience domestic abuse.

Being a domestic violence abuse victim hindered my career. It took over three years to resolve the divorce. The stress, worry, and anxiety took a toll on my mental health. I did not have the energy nor the cognitive ability to move up the corporate ladder. I was fortunate, though, because I had two huge advantages. The first is that I had, and still do, a tremendous support system. I do not know where I would be without my family and friends. The second advantage was that I kept working. At one point in my career, I considered leaving my job to stay home with my kids. Continuing to work, allowed me to walk away from an abusive relationship. I was still able to provide for my kids.

The divorce ruined me financially, however. I lost everything. I had to foreclose on my house, had no savings, and owed thousands and thousands of dollars to my attorney. I was broken and homeless. I ended up having to move in with my parents. My soul was in pain and shattered with little hope. I lost my home, my family, and was hanging on by a thread at work. I felt defeated and depleted.

Because we could not settle on custody of our kids, we ended up going to trial. Only 5% of divorce cases go to trial.[2] I was one of those cases. In the end, my ex-husband did not show up to the divorce trial. The court awarded

---

1   Martin R. Huecker, Kevin C. King, Gary A. Jordan, and William Smock; ed 7/25/21
2   SurviveDivorce.com

me full custody of my kids. The ordeal was finally over, and I could move on with my life. Thank goodness!

One day I woke up, and once again, I realized that I had the power to change my situation. I knew that I needed to rebuild. I needed to heal my spirit, take care of my mental health and fix my finances. I got to work! Eighteen months later, I was closing on a house.

Things were finally starting to turn around. I was the one making it happen. I realized that it was time to focus on my career again.

I worked in the insurance industry as an underwriter. I dreamed of being in management and playing a bigger role to lead the organization. Because I started focusing on my career, I improved from an average-rated employee to a top performer in one year! At the end of the year, I begin making inquiries about my career's next steps. I told one of the senior executives that I was interested in a management position. He said that he was happy I let him know my intentions because he would not have considered me for a management position. When I asked him why, he told me, "You never said anything." I realized at that moment that I must speak up for myself! You see, I had been working hard, head down in my cubicle, thinking that at any moment, someone is going to tap me on my shoulder and invite me to be a manager. However, nobody ever came. Once again, I realized that I had the power to change my future. For the first time in my life, I started campaigning for myself. Six months later, I finally stepped into a management role. I am now an Executive Vice President for a $50B global insurance company.

I aspire to live in a world where women will no longer have to deal with gender disparity in the workplace. Women are holding themselves back and are not even aware of it.

My mission is to raise women up in the world! I am doing that by sharing three lessons I learned while going through my divorce and career journey.

These three lessons have empowered me to succeed in my career and my life.

Lesson 1: Know That You Are Deserving

Women hold themselves back, by not believing that they deserve the career of their dreams. When you know that you deserve a fantastic job, you set yourself up for success.

Why is this important?

If you do not believe that you are worthy, you could fall into the 70% club. The Gallup World Poll stated that people are only engaged in their work 30% of the time. That leaves 70% of unhappy people at work.

Not believing that you are deserving, produces negative consequences:

- You do not enjoy your work.
- The days are long and dull.
- You see others getting promoted.
- You do not advance in your career.
- You do not get raises.
- Worst of all, you are not taking care of your family the way you want to with more income.

Once you know that you are deserving, everything changes. You become engaged in your work, which you enjoy. The days evaporate because you are no longer bored. Your manager recognizes your contributions, which is fulfilling. Best of all, you earn a promotion with a salary increase. The fact that you are happy also benefits your employer. Happy people at work are 12% more productive.[3]

How do you start to believe that you are deserving?

Identify your limiting beliefs. Why is it that you do not believe you are deserving? Why do you stay stuck in a dead-end job? Do you have the "I'll be happy when I get a new job" syndrome? Soul searching can help you

---

3   TheBalanceCareers.com

understand how and why you are holding yourself back. Once you find which beliefs are untrue and recognize how they limit you, you free yourself of that belief. You can then create a new outcome for your life. The power to change is attainable, when you believe that you are worthy.

Lesson one is to know that you are deserving.

Lesson 2: Embody a Growth Mindset

Another way to hold yourself back is by not embodying a growth mindset. Mindset refers to the way you think and react to life situations. Dr. Carol Dweck, a psychologist, named two distinct types of thinking: growth and fixed. You will miss opportunities to advance, if you stick with the fixed mindset, and you will suffer from the following consequences.

- You believe that people are against you.

- You do not take responsibility for your work quality.

- You blame others for your lack of advancement.

- You throw pity parties for yourself.

- You keep that unfulfilling job.

Whose fault is it then? Can you blame anyone for where you are in your career? The only person responsible is the person you see in the mirror every day. Shifting your thinking from a fixed mindset to a growth mindset is immensely powerful.

Why is this important?

It is because when you open your mind, you start to listen to what others are sharing with you. You can then receive the message and implement the recommendation. Listen, receive, and apply! Let me illustrate this. Let us assume that you get complaints about the quality of your work. Your manager schedules a meeting to give you feedback. They inform you that you need to improve your quality and give you suggestions. You walk away mad at the situation, not wanting to change your ways. This is an example of fixed thinking.

Applying a growth mindset to that same example produces a different result. You listened, implemented the advice, and the quality of your work improved! That is the power of a growth mindset.

Lesson two is to embody a growth mindset.

Lesson 3: Execute a Focused Strategy

Lack of focus is another way of holding yourself back. Joel A. Barker said, "Vision without action is merely a dream. Action without vision just passes the time. Vision with action can change the world." That quote is perfect to illustrate this lesson. Without the focus on your career, you are working hard but not seeing the results you wish. You see others promoted, but you are not. You try different things, but nothing is making a difference to get to that next level. The reason may be a lack of focus. Creating a focused strategy is a step-by-step plan to move you to the next level. I teach my clients to use a four-step process to execute their strategy.

1. **Aspire:** Be clear on what job you are pursuing. Pursue jobs or careers that bring you joy and passion.

2. **Assess:** Identify the concepts you need to develop. This could be working on your core values, mission, or vision. You can also find skills that you need to enhance to level up in your performance. Most importantly, work on your executive presence.

3. **Advice:** Ask your trusted colleagues to point out your areas of improvement. They can help you identify skills you do not know you need to enhance.

4. **Advertise:** Take the opportunity to network with leaders in your organization. Talk to them to let them know that you seek new opportunities. Ask them to share with you one piece of advice on how to earn a promotion.

When implemented well, a focused strategy will push you to the next level in your career.

Let me share with you a story about Cathy. She had a great attitude and good intentions to move up the corporate ladder. Cathy already believed that she was deserving and embodied a growth mindset. She had various ideas of projects she could work on to show her value and ability in her job. She kept talking about the work she was doing for weeks, but nothing ever materialized. Finally, I suggested that we sit down, so that I could see her progress. When she showed me her work, she was all over the place. She did not have a clear direction. She had different ideas started, but nothing finished. We outlined her four-step process, allowing her to gain momentum in her projects. She lacked a personal mission and vision that we created and ended up being her north star to figure out where to focus. Cathy generated solid projects, by layering the three principles which earned her a promotion with a salary increase.

Lesson three is to execute a focused strategy.

It is all coming together. By layering these three principles, you start to experience a compound effect. You now begin to figure out how to unlock the leader within!

The truth of my life is that being a domestic abuse violence victim was an unfortunate event. However, living through that made me stronger and resilient. I know I can empower myself, simply by applying these three lessons.

Now it is your turn to unleash the daredevil within and challenge yourself to get out of your comfort zone. You may not be asking someone out on a blind date, but you can go out there and get the job of your dreams and discover your truth. You are deserving!

Remember!

Be brave. Be bold. Take Action!

Rosie Zilinskas

Rosie Zilinskas is a leadership coach and expert in "Career Progression." She is an executive vice president specializing in high-net-worth personal insurance, with 29 years of experience climbing the corporate ladder.

Rosie is an international bilingual speaker, executive career coach, podcaster, author, and corporate trainer. She appeared on podcasts, such as "Bravehearts Radio," "The Driven Entrepreneur," and "Lead at any Level." She was also a featured storyteller at "The People Tree."

Rosie is the creator of the No Woman Left Behind 4-Step plan, which helps dozens of people obtain the promotion they sought to shred the frustration of a dead-end position.

Rosie is a first-generation Mexican American and fluent in Spanish. She is living proof that you really can have it all and move up the ladder of success despite the odds.

Rosie loves to read, travel, and spend time with family and friends. She resides in the Chicagoland area with her husband Ed and their 6-year-old mini — Golden Doodle Oakley. He has two incredible children, who are 23-year-old Bobby and 21-year-old Marissa.

Rosie Zilinskas
No Woman Left Behind
Orland Park, IL
630-346-2187
Rosie@NoWomanLeftBehind.com
www.NoWomanLeftBehind.com

No Woman Left Behind 4-Step Success Plan

Are you in corporate America and don't know why you are not moving up the corporate ladder?

Rosie's No Woman Left Behind 4-Step Success Plan video course will provide you with the strategy you need to figure out how you may be holding yourself back and how to overcome your barriers. When implemented correctly, the success plan will push you to the next level in your career.

This course will provide you with the road map of what to do next in your career to obtain the title and the money you deserve.

Scan the QR code to download your free course now.

https://Gift.NoWomanLeftBehind.com/Gift

Ann Papayoti

Becoming Buoyant

Life begins with an inhale and ends with an exhale. It's what happens in between that can leave us holding our breath.

My father taught me to swim at Cosby Lake, located in Clay, Alabama. Like many lakes, I recall the water being greenish-brown as if tinted by tea. We carefully walked hand in hand from the water's edge and into the surprisingly cool lake. Goosebumps emerged on my Coppertone lathered skin that was toasty warm from the southern sun. I hesitated as the water swelled around my ankles, and my toes squished into the slimy, mushy bottom. I felt myself sinking, and just in time, my daddy gently tugged, unsticking my feet that seemed held fast.

I feared the bottom of the lake. I thought it would swallow me up! The water appeared darker and murkier the further out we went. I clung to him, wrapped myself around his arm, and climbed his body like a tree until I was securely fastened to his back. With my arms around his neck, he lunged forward and swam as if we were one. He eventually found a spot away from others, unlaced my fingers, and lowered me into the water. He then carefully placed me on my back because *he insisted that I learned to float before I learned to swim*. With his encouraging words and supportive hands, I was able to relax, breathe intentionally and calmly, and stay afloat. I never knew he released his hold until he praised me. At first, I was startled and scared that I would sink. Instead, I remained buoyant — or something that resembled it — because I did not want to touch the bottom of the lake again.

I had no idea how important this lesson would be throughout my life.

My Dad did teach me to swim, and eventually, I became a competitive swimmer. I couldn't wait until I was old enough to become a lifeguard and spend my summers working at the community pool. It was a dream job to sit in the guard stand, twirl the whistle's lanyard around my hand, and watch the swimmers from behind my sunglasses, poised to pounce and assist anyone struggling in the water. In seven summers of lifeguarding, I did help a few. However, the training to prepare for those few times was intense. It was about survival — first and foremost, my own.

As I became a young adult, I recognized that life has a way of pulling us under. The first time I recall being pulled under, I was turning twenty years old. I was a university student and had my life planned out. I was all about structure — a list maker, box checker, first things first, step by step, sure-footed Capricorn high achiever. Until the breath was knocked out of me, deflating my plans, dreams, and every goal I had set for myself. You see, my best friends betrayed me. I lost my high school sweetheart, whom I expected to marry, and the girlfriend who was my closest confidant. I lost them to each other. It was like a great storm came up over me, knocking me out of my boat, into surging water, and leaving me fighting frantically to survive. However, the people I would have depended on to save me were the ones who had left me! *The ironic thing was they had first clung to me to save them in some way.*

I sunk into a sense of sadness and depression defined by plummeting self-esteem and confidence. I had a loss of direction, motivation, and life vision. It felt like guilt, embarrassment, hopelessness, disappointment, and grief. It sounded like self-hate, self-blame, self-doubt, and self-criticism. It looked like social withdrawal, health issues, weight gain, over-drinking, and academic failure. Until I touched the bottom because I hated that worse than I despised myself. Therefore, I tugged to loosen my feet, pushing and kicking, determined to reach the surface, get my head above water, exhale out this toxic mess and inhale in something, anything different. I immediately started swimming away from the old and toward the new — the closest boat. I chose to take responsibility for changing my life. I changed schools, made new friends, and got a job. In my new environment, I took care of myself, saved money, and began traveling. I got excited about my life!

The Next Storm

In my mid-twenties, I married a man who said everything I *needed* to hear about the betrayal by my best friends. He knew us all back when, and while I thought I had healed myself by pushing off the bottom and swimming away, clearly, I had not. His charismatic devotion and validating words filled holes and mended parts of me that were still battered and torn, yet well hidden behind masks of functionality and accomplishment.

Shortly into my marriage, I found myself overboard once again. I had completely lost myself because the man I loved was slowly chipping away at the very core of my being. His narcissistic manipulation left me confused, humiliated, and defeated. I was treading water in the weighty reality of my life, exhausted and on the verge of sinking. However, there was something inside me that refused to touch the bottom again.

Five years into the marriage, I recall curling under the covers after having sex with my husband. I wish I could say after making love, but that would be a lie. I prayed that I would not become pregnant. It was the first physical intimacy we had engaged in since the passing of our firstborn six months earlier. I hoped it would change. I hoped he would change. *Wouldn't everything be different now?* He seemed kinder — less strung out and emotionally volatile these past months. I was more than ready to have something besides the endless battering of grief to fill my days. However, the act was as it had been so many times before — crude, lacking love, connection, or even consideration. Verbal attacks began immediately after allowing him the permission he needed to leave for the evening and pursue whatever he had planned to entertain himself.

By this time, I'd stopped asking, *"How did I end up here?"* It seemed I had settled in some apathetic acceptance that this was my *"for better or worse"* commitment that I'd vowed before God and man. I saw no options. The truth is I found myself in a co-dependent relationship with fear. It was fear of embarrassing my family, fear of judgment from my Southern Baptist community, and fear of my husband — literally. This very secret and personal relationship with fear rendered me powerless and, therefore, stuck in an emotionally abusive, adulterous, and lonely marriage. I had become numb to the pain. It was like being in cold water too long — you no longer feel it.

It was late December 1994 and a holiday season to remember. My heart beat rapidly with anticipation of the future, and at the same time, a sense of dread. I held my right hand over my chest to contain what felt like an imminent explosion of my heart, and with tears blurring my vision, I struggled to refocus on the pregnancy test held in my left — it was positive.

The weight of this little plus sign brought me back to when my firstborn son was born prematurely and died at two weeks of age from colon complications. My body couldn't carry him full-term. I punished myself for this. I questioned if God was punishing me, too, for anything and everything I had ever done that wasn't good in His sight. I tried to blame God, the doctors, nurses, my job, my husband, the environment... but I always came back to me. It was *my* fault. It was my responsibility to nurture, protect and deliver him safely into this world, and I had failed.

AND NOW I WAS terrified! My first thought was *I might fail another child.* I felt myself sink until the excruciating pain from the effort of screaming underwater jolted my consciousness. My thought immediately shifted to, *I am drowning in this marriage, but I will not allow MY child to DROWN WITH ME.*

This child, whom I had first prayed would not come to be, NOW became my reason for survival. After four months, I went into premature labor and was admitted to the hospital to avoid another premature birth. They didn't give me much hope, but I was determined not to fail. After four more long months of inversion bed rest, IVs, catheters, sleep deprivation, and continual contractions, I was blessed to receive the gift of my son.

What we cannot do for ourselves, we can do for others, especially our kids, right? The tables began to turn as I found the courage to speak up and stand up. I used my newfound voice to set expectations and boundaries, even though I was laughed at and spat on. I saw an opportunity to get involved with training facilitation at work, applied, and interviewed. I got the gig. I went from surviving to striving to change my path and create more for myself, and in turn, for my son. I was respected and applauded for my contributions and talents. I was being reminded of who I was before the betrayal and before the needy heart. I was someone who could balance empathy with accountability and lead others naturally. I was dependable, kind, and creative. And *enough*.

Once I started feeling like myself again, I wanted more of me and less of him. In fact, I wanted to fully revive my life. There was no denying I was not free to be me in my marriage. What was still lacking was the courage to get out. However, like all who choose change, there is a cross-point moment in time of both being *ready* and the *opportunity* to do something. I would have to rescue myself. *But how?*

I finally stopped holding my breath and surfaced, which was a tremendous relief. Yet, it seemed like I was juggling while treading water. I was still coping with and tolerating much as I struggled with fully letting go.

Release Your Fear

When I was a teenager in lifeguard training, I didn't have to learn to juggle while treading water. However, I did have to tread water until I was fatigued while fully dressed, creating an extra heavy burden. I learned to conserve my energy to allow me to meet the time requirement without panicking, giving up, or wearing out. I also learned to shed my weighty wardrobe and create a flotation device from one piece of clothing by filling it with air while staying upright. Even though I would feel vulnerable, I would have to allow the remaining items to simply fall away. I learned to let my body and my mind rest, float, and relax. I learned to be still, to trust my device and silence the thoughts that would create fear, doubt, or worry, and embrace the gift of buoyancy, breath, and calm.

This time to rest, recharge my body, and rejuvenate my mind would allow me the focus and energy to succeed in the next thing, the next drill, or the next test that was certain to come. Suddenly, I'd be presented with an emergency situation and would need to fill my lungs with oxygen before *purposefully diving under to rescue a victim*. Had I not conserved energy, dedicated time to rest my body and mind, dropped some of the weight I was wearing, the burden I was carrying, I would have been no help to them and likely would have drowned us both. *I also had to know when to let go of the other person and save myself.* To leave my marriage, I would have to strip away my fear, inflate my confidence, and allow myself to float.

Just like Daddy said, "Float first." I could then choose a direction to swim with strength and clarity.

Recover Your Truth, Revive Your Life

Do you ever feel like you're juggling while treading water? That life is pulling you under, and you are sinking to the bottom? Are you stuck in a cycle of pain? A pattern of abuse? Of self-sabotage? Have you been holding your breath, waiting for something or someone to change? Are you asking how you got here? *Does your life need resuscitating?*

Many people struggle to break free from the way they are living their life. They typically run or *swim* away, as I once did, to the closest boat seeking external validation while avoiding healing. However, the key to breaking free and reviving an authentic life is not by running or swimming away. It requires you to stop, admit that you are not okay, and float for a while. It is only in this stillness that you can open your airway, rescue your breath, restart your heart, and fully recover.

I now help others revive their lives by **connecting the dots** of their journey, **pinpointing the pain** that keeps them stuck, and **recovering the truth** of who they are, so that they can let go and live freely. I guide people through this process I call **Soul CPR**.

By connecting the dots like on the child's menu in a restaurant, a clear picture emerges of how you got to where you are. It is often surprisingly different than what you imagined it would be. This new awareness helps pinpoint the pain that has kept you struggling in and underwater. Once you identify and understand your self-sabotaging and limiting thoughts, emotions, behaviors, and habits, you'll stop denying your true self. You will be ready to recover the truth of who you are and align your life so that you thrive once more. *You will restore your soul.*

Beyond the initial betrayal, the death of my son, and since leaving my abusive marriage, there has been much that could have sunk me: single parenting, post-divorce custody battle, transitioning careers at midlife, multiple relocations, rebuilding communities, youngest child's health + learning + social struggles, my parents' deaths, my sister-in-law's suicide, my own physical health crisis, my foster daughter's mental health and lifestyle choices... to name a few. I am sure many of you have quite a laundry list as well!

Research repeatedly finds that experiencing even one emotionally traumatic event *without building a healing resilience* can have a devastating long-term impact on overall well-being and life satisfaction. Our health and happiness are directly anchored to untangling from our past and healing our hearts!

People ask me how I survive. My answer is, I stop. Float. Rest. Listen. Reflect. Feel. Cry, and sometimes Scream, but from the surface. I refuse to hold my breath and be pulled down into the heart-stopping, emotional quicksand. I face the truth, trust myself, own my voice, let go of who and what I must, and navigate each experience following my own North Star.

There will always be more storms, painful moments, and challenges to overcome. Winds of uninvited change and mighty waves of grief will threaten and test you. However, when you are strong in who you are and where you are headed, you will navigate your life accordingly and not be led off course, thrown overboard, or pulled under. You will be *unsinkable.*

The lesson is always about letting go, isn't it?

Ann Papayoti

Ann Papayoti has always been the go-to girl for friends experiencing problems. She could have started her own "Dear Annie" column decades ago! In fact, her high school yearbook quotes a classmate describing her as a "good listener." Little did she know then that listening with empathy was an invaluable, innate skill that would become foundational to her life's work.

Ann is the founder of SkyView Coaching. She is an international life, leadership, and relationship coach, speaker, writer, educator, and co-author of The Gift of Shift, an intimate self-help book.

She is an Expert Contributor for YourTango Media and has been featured in MSN, Google, Yahoo, Apple News, and more. Ann has spoken at conferences, summits, and commemorations, both live and online, throughout North America. She captivates, educates, and inspires audiences by sharing her personal experiences of loss, transition, and triumph.

Ann helps people rise above life's painful and challenging moments, so they can revive their life and thrive once more. She is known for the personal and compassionate way she guides people to their own insights and growth, having helped thousands of people with their personal and professional goals.

Her credentials include a B.A. in Journalism and Communications and multiple professional certifications, including Certifed Professional Coach (CPC), Master Energy Leadership Index Practitioner (ELI-MP), and NeuroLinguistics Programming Practitioner (NLP).

Ann currently resides in a charming little town near Dallas, Texas, with her family. This almost empty-nester rises and shines each morning by teaching group fitness classes before beginning her workday. With a love of dance since childhood, Zumba is her passion, along with loaded-lattes and page-turner books.

To learn how she can help you or to book her for an event, connect with Ann on her website, Facebook, or Instagram.

Ann Papayoti
SkyView Coaching
Grapevine, TX
214-596-8044
Ann@SkyViewCoaching.com
https://SkyViewCoaching.com
www.Facebook.com/SkyViewCoaching
www.Instagram.com/AnnPapayoti
www.Amazon.com/dp/1663211256

Photography by Erika Hanchar.

Step-by-Step Soul CPR

If you have experienced emotional trauma, perhaps you can relate to the need to recover your breath and revive your heart. Ann's complimentary video guide and downloadable workbook provides a step-by-step process for you to restore your soul.

Whether you are in it or beyond it, you will gain invaluable personal insight from this process.

Scan the QR code or visit her website to get started!

https://SkyViewCoaching.com/soul-cpr-free-gift

Karolyn Wotring

From We to Me

It all started with my little, 4 foot 1-inch momma!

My dad died of cancer when I was only two, and my mom, a stay-at-home wife who had never worked outside of the home, was left with **SIX KIDS.**

Unfortunately, being two when he died, I don't remember much about my dad. I do remember how tough things were for my mom at times and how much she inspired me.

My Mom is a ROCKSTAR...

I can remember when she worked two jobs and bought her own home, so we would always have a roof over our heads. We always had food to eat, even if a few times it was delivered in a box from a local charity.

My mom did her best to give us the things that we needed, but she wasn't always able to give us everything we wanted. Life doesn't work that way. I also learned that I had the ability to work for the things that I wanted. As soon as I was old enough, I started working. I babysat, worked at a hot dog stand, and a pizza place. When I was 16 years old, I got a job bussing tables at a fancy french restaurant. I worked hard at that job and paid for my own college tuition. I went to school all day, came home, did my homework, and then worked in the evenings so that I would have extra money to buy the things that I wanted.

I recall one-day delivering salads to one of my tables; just after I set down the second plate, a man at the table gave me this awful, cold look. He then abruptly leaned over, sighed loudly, looked me square in the eye, and with the most rigid voice I had ever heard said, "IF YOU DON'T LIKE YOUR JOB, GET OUT!"

WOW!!! I remember the sting in my eyes and my whole body freezing. I gave him a slight nervous nod and practically ran back to the server station to hide. As soon as I made it around the corner, I burst into tears. I was only 16 years old, and having been raised by a single mom most of my life, I was not used to being spoken to like that by a man. I took a few moments to calm myself down, and when I was finally brave enough to go back out into the dining room, I glanced over, and the same man was now waving me back to his table. My heart sank. All I was thinking was, what did I do???

I timidly approached the table, and this time he leaned in toward me, gave me a warm, soft smile, and he spoke something that I would never forget. "I didn't say that to hurt you," he said to me. "I said it to help you. You see, That may have been the 20th plate that you put down tonight, but it's the first one that you put down in front of my wife. You can choose to do a job that you don't enjoy, or you can do something that you love and do it with complete joy. I want you to remember three things.

1. You are smart enough to learn anything you want to learn.

2. You can have anything you want in this world if you put your mind to it.

3. Never ever let anyone intimidate you into not going for what you want."

Then he reached out and discretely placed something into my hand.

I am often asked what makes me so passionate about what I do. It's simple. I absolutely love helping women. I believe in my heart that our lives are what we create them to be. We can sit around and wait for things to "get better," or we can take charge, dream dreams, set goals, and create a plan for an amazing future. I often tell my clients and friends that this is just a chapter you are going through. The rest of the book is yours. *Be the author of the next chapters of your story. Create a life you love. Create your own sunshine!*

My mom is now 85. A few years ago, I asked her if there was one thing that she would have liked to do that she has not yet fulfilled. She's still thinking about it, but the question got me thinking about how I wanted to write my next chapters.

For me, my biggest wants and dreams have always revolved around traveling and cooking...

One thing that I've always wanted to do is go to Italy and have someone's grandma teach me how to make fresh pasta.

Just after my divorce, my youngest was away at college, and I thought it was the perfect time to do something for just me. I worked with my friend and travel agent Tracey, and I made my dream a reality.

I took my "Eat Pray Love, trip." Twelve days, solo, across the Italian countryside. Honestly, there was not much praying or loving going on, but the eat part, I had that down! As Julia Roberts would say, there was NO CARB LEFT BEHIND!!!

I rode my bicycle through the Tuscan countryside to a vineyard for a Chianti tasting. I toured Rome on a Segway. I learned that Italy has something called Scooterino, which is like Uber, but Italian men come and pick you up on a scooter and take you to your destination. I took six cooking classes from Florence to the Amalfi coast. One class was taught on a rooftop in Rome at dusk, overlooking St. Peter's Basilica.

I Was Writing My Next Chapter

The highlight of my journey was the three days that I stayed in an 18th-century boutique hotel and biodynamic vineyard called Palazzo Trinconi, which was in a small cliff town in the heart of Ciociaria, Lazio, about an hour south of Rome. There was nothing touristy about Arce, but it was an amazing way to emerse myself in the culture. I learned to make pizza from a fun and very charming Italian young chef named Giuseppe, and yes, of course, I learned to make the most amazing fresh and authentic pasta from an Italian grandmother. Mille didn't speak a word of English, but we made fettucine, ravioletti, and gnocchi through an interpreter. We cooked, drank wine, and I relished every moment of this amazing experience. I remembered the words and life lesson that a very firm but kind man said 29 years earlier.

1. You are smart enough to learn anything you want to learn.

2. You can have anything you want in this world if you put your mind to it.

3. Never ever let anyone intimidate you into not going for what you want.

By the way, reader... if you're wondering what he put in my hand that day, it was a very crisp $100 bill. That was a pretty big deal for a 16-year-old girl in 1987. (I think he felt bad for making me cry. That man will never know how much I still value that powerful lesson that he imparted on me that day.)

What does all this mean for you? I want to help every one of you to become the author of your next chapters. I want to help you identify your hopes and dreams and help you to build a financial plan to make each of those dreams an achievable reality. Each of you is on your own journey right now. Whether you are single, married, a widow, or a divorcee, the future is yours to create. I would love to be your guide to your best life.

As a financial advisor for over three decades, a Certified Divorce Financial Analyst, and the creator of the Financially Savvy Woman, I believe that every woman needs to know the essential fundamentals to being financially savvy.

We will touch on a few of them here, and I will tell you about how we used the FSW fundamentals to help some of my clients write their next chapters.

Fundamental #1
A Financially Savvy Woman Knows Her Numbers

You MUST know what comes in and what goes out each month. Ignorance is NOT bliss when it comes to financial planning. It would help if you thought of your household like a business. No successful business would work without a cash flow. This can be achieved with the FSW cash flow worksheet, which is available on my website. Money is like time. If you have no plan, it is often wasted.

Sara — Spender's Guilt

Sara's challenge was that she didn't really understand what she had or what she needed, so rather than enjoying life, she was super frugal and lived with spender's guilt.

Sara worked as an administrative assistant most of her life. When I met her, she was 68 and still working. She spent all her working years taking care of the needs of her employer and the company, and she never took the time to learn about how to best plan for her own future. She has always been a good saver. She contributed to her company's 401k and had a pension from one of her jobs. She knew that she was eligible for social security in retirement, but she wasn't quite sure at what age she should begin taking it. One of Sara's biggest concerns was not running out of money. She'd shared that she'd like to leave a little something to her family, but she also knew that she would most likely be on her own in retirement. She wanted to be sure that she planned for Long Term Care so that she would never be a burden to her family. Sara and I worked through our financially savvy cash flow, and we were able to identify her monthly financial need. We then built a plan that she could see on paper. I showed her how each year we would strategically use the different "Time Buckets" of money to replace her income and even give her an extra "Fun Bucket" that she could use for all the extra things that she would like to do in retirement. Before working with me, Sara always felt a bit guilty spending money or going on trips because she was concerned that she didn't have enough. Knowing that we had carefully considered everything, including implementing the best tax strategies, Sara was now able to have the freedom to enjoy spending some of her hard-earned money guilt-free. She is going on trips to see her family, and she is truly enjoying her retirement to the fullest.

Fundemental #2
She Begins With A Strong Foundation

A financially savvy woman plans for the bad times as well as the good times. She knows that she must have a very clear understanding of what she has, what she needs, and what is available to her now and in the future. She must have a strong foundation before she is able to build her dream life.

Mary — Alone and Unsure

Mary and Ted had spent their married life together, planning for the day they would retire and travel. Unfortunately, Ted had passed away the day before his 61st birthday. Ted's passing left Mary alone to navigate her finances and life on her own. One of my clients introduced me to Mary about four months after Ted passed. Mary shared with me that Ted was a hard-working man, and he left her with a military pension as well as another small pension from a previous employer. They both had 401k's and life insurance policies that helped cover final expenses. Just after Ted's passing, Mary had contacted the social security office, but not knowing "the right questions" to ask, she was given the $250 death benefit and was told that she makes too much money to collect survivor benefits and was sent her on her way. Mary and I used a FSW Strategy session to carefully map out time buckets for Mary. Considering taxes as well as restrictions from social security, we were able to generate a comfortable stream of income shortly after our first meeting. Mary is now comfortably retired and enjoying life with her kids and grandkids and making the most of the legacy that Ted left for all of them.

Fundamental #3
A Financially Savvy Woman Has an Educated/Trusted Advisor

It's great if you have a friend or family member that you look up to as a financial mentor. It is critically important that you work with someone who works as a fiduciary. A fiduciary is someone that holds proper financial licenses, is educated in finance, and puts your needs and goals above their own. Your financial planner should have an ongoing relationship with you. Together you should review and update your plan annually at minimum, most importantly, when your life or situation changes. Your advisor should know your total picture and understand your goals. A financially savvy woman uses a true holistic planner who educates her along the way and helps to build confidence in her financial knowledge.

Kim — Beaten Down and Scared

Kim was a dynamic young girl that bravely came to America over 30 years prior to meeting me. She is one of the most kind-hearted women that I know. Kim came to the U.S. from Japan as a nanny when she was just barely 21. She met her husband Steve and was married to him for 31 years. Kim let Steve take the lead on all of the financial matters, and then one day, he came to her and told her that he didn't want to be married to her anymore. He told her that she should go back to Japan because she didn't know anything about money and that no matter how much he gave her, she would blow it.

Kim and I worked very closely using the FSW CDFA (Certified Divorce Financial Analyst) fundamentals to build a plan for her portion of the marital assets and a monthly plan for her independent life going forward. I took a lot of time to make sure that she understood our plan and educated her little by little.

Each year, while doing her annual review, I am so proud of the strong understanding she now has of her finances and how her money is working for her. She is confident with her financial security and is no longer uneducated. She is empowered and now holds her head up high, knowing that she no longer needs anyone else to care for her.

Life is a journey. Right now, you may be going through one of youe most difficult times. I am here to guide you, educate you, and empower you to be The Financially Savvy Woman that you want to be. You are not alone! You don't need to know everything. It would be best to find someone you trust to guide you and teach you how to reach your own financial security. Will you let me be that person for you?

I have included an opportunity for you to learn more. Begin writing your next chapter. Visit the link below to receive a complimentary digital copy of The 7 Financially Savvy Strategies. You may also book a complementary Financially Savvy Strategy session directly on my calendar by following the link.

When I was a little girl, my mom used to call me "Winnie." So, I will leave you with the words of Christopher Robin.

"Promise me you'll always remember:
You're braver than you believe,
and stronger than you seem,
and smarter than you think."

Karolyn Wotring

Karolyn Wotring ("Watch-Ring") is an influencer, a leader of women, and a recipient of the Chicagoland 2016 Woman of Distinction award.

As a financial planner, she has managed hundreds of millions of dollars in financial assets and is the personal financial advisor to many top executives at Fortune 500 companies like Grainger, Abbott Laboratories, and LinkedIn. Karolyn is proud of the stability and independence that she is able to bring to her clients by helping them not only to grow their assets but also to protect their financial future with a great foundation of Life Insurance and Long-Term Care.

She has spent three decades working as a financial advisor with Investment firms large enough to sponsor Major sporting events such as the most famous golf tournament and football game of the year. As the Founder of The Financially Savvy Woman, Karolyn is one of only 2% of all Financial planners that has earned the distinct title of Certified Divorce Financial Analyst.

After her father's death at two years old, Karolyn was raised by a single mom of six kids. Her mom worked two jobs and taught her early that if you work hard, you can rise above your situation and succeed.

As a leader and host of the Illinois Women of Influence group and a mom of two children of her own, Karolyn has helped thousands of women succeed with their goals and truly be Financially Savvy Women.

Karolyn Wotring CDFA®
The Financially Savvy Woman
Boca Raton, FL
847-772-3829
Karolyn.Wotring@nm.com
KarolynWotring.nm.com

Financially Savvy Strategy Session

Are you ready to create the life that you want for yourself? The first step is to know what it takes to be financially savvy.

Contact Karolyn to set up a complimentary 15-minute strategy session where she will answer any questions that you may have about making smart choices with your money.

KarolynWotring.NM.com

Dennis Mellen

B.E.A.N. Roadmap

I slowly awaken from what feels like a wine-induced stupor to face a bright shining light directly in my face. As I try to make my eyes focus, I am thinking, "Could the lights be any brighter? Am I being interrogated by the FBI or police? What did I do?" As if on cue, my eyes come into focus, and I lock eyes with my brother standing over me with tears streaming down both cheeks. I smile and say, "Hey butthead." He laughs and says, "Dennis, you had us soooooo scared." That was me coming back to reality. A vague memory comes to mind of mountain biking on a trail East of Seattle aptly named in the trail guide as "It's A Bitch"… IAB for short.

The trail description reads, "The first trail to the larger trail system is called IAB (It's A Bitch)." IAB does live up to its name as you bike/hike 1 mile and gain 500ft. However, once at the top, there are no more big climbs. The trails are all rolling fun, and technical. "The Iron Man" portion seems to be that first mile.

Decked out in fairly conservative bike shorts, a dry-fit shirt, black helmet, and gray bike shoes, I'm not one of those bikers festooned like a Nino Baldacci from the Italian biking team. Have you seen some of those guys? I mean, come on! They make Mardi Gras revelers look like they're dressed business casual.

Looking for the trailhead, I pass some of the King County Park System yurts used for camping. I make reference for a future camping trip possibility, even though my wife's idea of camping is a three-star hotel. Maybe my sons might be interested.

The yurt area is all neatly trimmed back, but the beginning point of IAB is blocked by green undergrowth. After a couple of fruitless sallies into dead-ends behind several yurts, I spy the trail leading off to the north with a long steady climb under some tall Douglas firs and what the trail guide describes as verdant undergrowth. (I think the last time I used the word "verdant" was studying for college, but I digress.)

The forest canopy is thick, blocking a lot of the sunlight, with bright yellow shafts of light streaming through intermittently. The trail is wet and filled with pine needles, looking like a scene from Star Wars. Any minute, I'm expecting a speeder to come by with a Stormtrooper, or even Luke Skywalker, at the wheel.

On the next switchback, the incline changes dramatically. I am forced to the lowest gear. My speed drops to that of a circus performer riding a unicycle. I can feel my lungs burn. However, I'm loving it because of the challenge. To jump off the bike and walk, well, that's for wieners.

Today, I'm determined to be a WINNER, make it non-stop to the top of IAB as the steepness lessens for about a quarter of a mile. The trail leads back westward, away from the edge of the hill. I think a drink of water would be nice, but that would require a stop. Through my conflicting thoughts, I ask, but who am I racing? There's nobody else on the trail. They are all working today, and I am a lucky, mid-week day off, professional airline captain with an FAA Class I physical trying to stay healthy.

I round a curve near the top, and I'm working myself very hard. My breath comes in controlled gasps and then uncontrollable huffs. However, I'm almost to the top — no time to let up now. Only a less manly man would do that. I feel the sweat sweeping down my back, bringing waves of wetness. Sweat is dripping from my eyebrows and my wrists. My gloves are soaked. I can see a clearing ahead and a blue sky above me.

Maybe I should take a water break. Maybe I should sit down and look across the valley to the river below. After all, the trail description says it's only a mile and a 500-foot elevation climb, and I'm almost there anyway. Nobody will know I rested. I stop, swing my leg over the rear wheel, and take a couple of steps. Man, I need to sit down.

Finding a log, I let my bike fall over, and I settle on a mossy black tree trunk, cradling my chin in my hands, my elbows on my knees. For some reason, I have an urge to lay down. Nearby voices are saying something unintelligible. I roll to my knees and promptly projectile vomit the contents of my stomach, and quite possibly pass out. I don't know. I don't know what's happening... I don't know...

The main gist of the story continues from one day being literally on top of the world flying at 35,000 feet as a 30 plus year professional pilot through the devastating, no, the crushing loss of my pilot license.

All I ever wanted to do was be a professional pilot. You see, I had what I call an inverted life, unlike most 18-year-old high school grads. I was wondering what I was going to do now, job, college, next school. I HAD A SINGLENESS IN PURPOSE, to have a lifelong career as a professional pilot. So, how'd I get there?

At age 10, living at my father's Air Force base, I saw airplanes flying overhead and thought, "Hey, that's pretty cool, that's what I want to do when I grow up." Of course, my wife says I've never reached that point, but we won't talk about it.

From 10 years old to 56 years old, I never had a single thought of doing anything else. They say if you love your job, you'll never work a day of your life. My close friends claim I've never worked a day, period.

So, what do you do when you have a serious heart attack? Is there another kind? What if you have a health issue that changes your whole life when you lose a career where you never felt you worked a day in your life, a career or season-ending athletic injury, or a business failure? How do you recapture your purpose so that you can delay the arrival of Geezerville? You know Barcalounger, cool drink, remote, and Oprah re-runs.

Just my recovery, finding a purpose is what engages you or an employee. Purpose is what gets and keeps employees engaged, but it is hard to measure engagement. Disengagement rears its head in absenteeism, turnover, and retraining costs. It costs you $18,000 for every $100,000 of payroll. That is a lot of money, and you, as a leader, are the biggest influencer of engagement.

Your current culture and leadership you've established are perfect for the results you are getting right now. However, if you are not satisfied with your results, your leadership is the first place to look to improve. Leaders are the single biggest influencer of culture. A leader is the connection between the vision and the culture. What can you do?

I've come up with an acronym to help you get started. It is a road map, if you will, to help your team change challenges into opportunities using the **B.E.A.N.** acronym. You ask where the **B.E.A.N.** acronym came from. My story behind it goes like this. The business environment is an ever-present constant roiling, boiling pot of water. The boiling water represents events coming at you. Each event has an outcome. If we choose to do nothing, then we accept whatever the outcome is. However, if we choose to react, we choose to affect the outcome.

The business challenges never stop coming at you, and you, as a leader, are like a coffee bean. As a bean, your experiences, what you learned through the University of Hard Knocks, is like going through the roasting and grinding process. As a positive leader, you are the bean in the brewing process. You change the surrounding water into gourmet coffee that smells good, tastes good, and positively changes the water. You, as a leader, can be that coffee bean and influence the outcome of events.

So, how can you be a bean with your team? Let's look at **B.E.A.N.**

B

Begin... the hardest step in any journey is the first. Remember when you were a kid and went bowling for the first time? Despite your protests, they put the gutter bumpers up. You would roll the ball, and most likely, the ball would bump against the bumpers a couple of times. However, you got some pins as you got better. You got more pins and less bumper until eventually, you could bowl without the bumpers and maybe even get a good score. However, if you never rolled the ball, you would never get any pins. BEGIN, ROLL YOUR BALL.

E

Execute your plan. Anyone can have a plan. A plan is just a plan, unless you execute it. There's a story about three crows sitting on the fence overlooking a cornfield. One crow decides to fly south. How many crows are left on the fence? Three, because there's a difference between deciding and doing. Knowing the plan ain't doing the plan! Too many people know all about how to make plans but never execute and then exercise their: could've, should've, would've, regret cycle of armchair quarterbacking. EXECUTE your plan.

A

The "A" of **B.E.A.N.** stands for adapting to the volatility, uncertainty, complexity, and ambiguity of events. You must adapt to the events of the ever-changing situation happening. A former world boxing champion, Mike Tyson, was asked what he did when his fight plan was not working. He said, "Everybody GOT a plan, until they get punched in the face. You got to adjust." It's a realization that your plan needs to adapt, and it isn't working. It needs to be altered because the new information or changing circumstances occur like you got punched in the face. When you ADAPT, you use the new feedback, your experience, and new data as you receive it. It is often like a stinging punch to the face, that makes you adjust to challenges, so you can affect the outcome.

N

Finally, the N of **B.E.A.N.** is, "Take care of the next 200 feet on your journey." If you take a trip from Chicago to Disney World, you can go through Memphis, Knoxville, Nashville, or every which way you want. Some are faster, have better scenery, and some require detours. However, they all get to your goal of Disney World. Just like driving at night, where your headlights only cover about 200 feet, you need to take care of the next 200 feet and then the next 200 feet, until you eventually reach your "Disney World." Always take care of the NEXT 200 feet, while keeping your goal in mind.

B.E.A.N. did not come to me right away, and I always learn the hard way anyway. It came as an afterthought. It became a roadmap of how to influence the roiling, boiling pot of water that is business and competition.

Business is a very dynamic environment. **B.E.A.N.** is only a guide, a needed roadmap. Do you ever say, "I never face challenges, and I am totally satisfied with my performance, right?" All my orders arrive on time, my culture is great, no quarantines, no irate customers, everything goes as planned, no surprises, right? Don't we wish? **B.E.A.N.** gives you a starting point.

In addition to being an author, I also do positive leadership training for teams and 1-on-1 leadership coaching. I help team leaders from large and small businesses engage their employees, reduce absenteeism, turnover, and retraining costs. To find out details on the leadership training, scan the QR code on the following page or go to www.BeABean.net and schedule a discovery call. My team will send you Four Actionable Items that you can use today to Be A Bean.

With this **B.E.A.N.** roadmap, go Be A Bean, jump into the boiling water, take care of what's important now and transform your team or your challenges from ordinary water into gourmet coffee. Get your team to perform at a level that you never thought possible. Connect the culture with the vision.

Dennis Mellen

Dennis Mellen, a Jon Gordon Certified Positive Leadership Trainer, Consultant, and Author of "Takes More Than Heart; Changing the Journey's Challenges into Opportunities," brings years of business experience in the airline industry, military, consulting, teaching, and coaching, including 28 years at Alaska Airlines flying, building training programs, and leading teams of over 550 pilots and 40 instructors. These experiences provide insightful stories to connect his audience to the foundations for building relationships, connecting with people, and engaging teams in their vision and purpose.

Dennis focuses on helping each organization, team, and individual build more positive mindsets, teams, and cultures. With worldwide presentations in such places as Kenya, the Philippines, and Cape Verde, Dennis emphasizes how diverse views can lead to innovation and new ideas. Positive leaders are like coffee beans as they go through the roiling, boiling, brewing process of business. Be A Bean and change your team from ordinary water into gourmet coffee.

Dennis is a business leader, motivator, mental performance mentor, and a passionate, athletic coach. Enthusiastic leadership and followership are his trademarks. He brings a high level of energy and passion to every group he engages. Weaving personal anecdotes and experiences with specific calls to action are key elements in his presentations.

Dennis Mellen
Be A Bean
Algonquin, IL
DennisMellen@hotmail.com
https://BeABean.net

The Power of Positive Leadership Training

Create a culture of positive leadership! Let's schedule a discovery call and talk about the Power of Positive Leadership Training presented by Dennis Mellen. Dennis and his team will send you Four Actionable Items you can use today to inspire your team.

In this training, you will learn the proven strategies Jon Gordon teaches millions, coupled with the real-life experiences and heart of Dennis. At this virtual or live training, you will learn how to create a company culture that not only scales for more profit but thrives under ANY condition! Turn your team into an unstoppable force! Get your team to perform at a level no one thought possible.

www.BeABean.net/4-actionable-steps

Margie Dunki-Jacobs

Stand Up! Speak Your Truth!

"Butter!" The command came from my husband's uncle, Joe, as we sat down to a beautifully and thoughtfully prepared hot meal in front of us. His sweet wife, Leslie, had worked all afternoon to set an inviting table, pick flowers from the garden and make iced tea garnished with fresh mint and lemons in a glass pitcher. She made fresh hot rolls from scratch and prepared a lovely sauteed chicken with mushrooms and sides of mashed potatoes and green beans. How could anyone feel anything but enormous gratitude for the person who had prepared all of this in love for others to enjoy. After Joe led us in the blessing over the food, the first word out of his mouth was a stern "Butter!" It wasn't on the table. I have always been a helpful person, so I said, "I'll get it." He said only her first name, "Leslie!"

Three years into my marriage to such a kind man, I couldn't imagine my husband treating me that way — ever. I watched in disbelief as my aunt jumped from the table, apologized, ran, and got the butter like a frightened little mouse, brought it to the table, put her head down, and apologized one more time, as he cleared his throat as if to make a point that he was in control. We ate while having awkward, meaningless small talk.

It's the reason I'm still married to the same person after 38 years. I decided *at that moment* I would always use my voice to speak what was on my mind and speak my truth. Our relationship would be open and communicative. I decided *at that moment* that nobody was going to push me down and intimidate me in the way that I witnessed, not just that once, but over and over throughout the years of knowing him. He never laid a hand on her. He didn't have to. He had destroyed her self-worth to the point that she felt she didn't deserve to speak up. If she did, his harsh words would devastate her, and she learned to settle for "good enough." Was settling for "good enough" the dream for her life?

To the outside world, everything looked perfect. They'd smile in photos together and manage life together. However, the bickering on the inside of the home was from sun-up to sundown because Leslie, may she rest in peace, was too afraid to speak up. After Joe passed, I had two really amazing and wonderful years getting to know the real Leslie. The drama was gone. Don't let the drama pull you in. Calmly remove yourself from it, and let others know confidently that you will not be a part of it. There's no time for it. Every day we have here is to be cherished and lived fully. One day cannot be wasted, let alone a decade or a lifetime.

It's not uncommon to be taught in your younger years to "bite your tongue." When you do that, you don't allow yourself to have a voice. You don't allow the real *you* to evolve and create new growth, so that you can live the joyful, healthy life you are wanting for yourself. You may stay stifled by being quiet, and before you know it, you've settled for less than because it's easier. You convince yourself that things are good enough. What if the advice given to us along the way had been, "Never be afraid to speak your truth. Always stand up for what you believe in." As the famous and endearing Les Brown teaches us, "Don't let anyone else's opinion become your reality." Never let anyone control you. If you find yourself in a relationship that has signs of being unhealthy, leave at the moment you know that. Walk out the door. Don't look back. Backward is not an option. Know that your life is worthy of love, respect, and joy. My wish for you is to always live in a healthy and safe environment.

You know that the direction of your life is forward. You have dreams, ideas, and aspirations. Take responsibility for yourself. When you are willing to take yourself to the next level of achieving your dreams, you will put yourself on the path of success, moving forward, breathing forward, and stepping forward in excitement, commitment, and passion.

In 2017, I created a retreat day for women called Breathing Forward at the University of Vermont. The first attendees were extraordinary. I gathered their love and ideas and founded my empowerment company that same year, Breathing Forward, LLC. I left the workforce the following year to start a new chapter of my life as an inspirational speaker, author, and business success coach.

I plugged in with high-level coaches, threw the bulk of my savings into learning from the best, and never looked back. In my first book, "Overly Satisfied is Underachieved," I talk about how to stop settling for "good enough" and start getting what you "really want." It is important to me to walk the walk. It led me into coaching others one-on-one and in groups. From there, I've seen the need to produce masterclasses and online courses to help raise people above the line and intentionally live above the line! What's the line, you ask? It's more impactful if you do it. Grab a blank white sheet of paper and draw a horizontal line across the page mid-way. Below the line, list the things that have happened in your past that you no will longer tolerate. Everything you can think of. Above the line, list all the things you are committing to and where you are taking your life! If you stop and take time to do this exercise, I promise you it will change your life. Don't ever let anyone push you below the line. You are strong, someone with a desire to create greatness for you and your family. Say out loud, "I commit to living my best life above the line."

When you partner with someone or marry someone, they have dreams and ideas of their own. In a partnership, it's not about having one person decide which direction you should go and the other one passively listening. This is your _only_ life. You have a say in it, and in fact, your voice of truth is the most powerful of all! You have been given the gift of knowing which direction you want to go inside your soul, so tap into that. It's easy to get confused along the way and lose your direction through circumstances that happen to us or "for us." However, that doesn't mean you're lost. It's always okay to reach out for guidance, for friendships to support you, and for coaches who have a higher depth of understanding. It's not uncommon to allow someone in our lives whom we may love at the time or think that we love, point us in a different direction than we want to go. When it doesn't align with who you are, let go of the "bite your tongue" thinking and step into your belief, faith, strength, and boldness! Surround yourself with people who will lift you up, rather than hold you down.

This chapter is for you if you have ever decided it was better to stand in silence as an unhappy person and not make waves rather than take a stand for yourself and create your happiness.

Take a stand for yourself. Create your happiness. If you haven't had the courage to break the chains that are holding you back from living your best life, it starts with a decision, followed by a commitment. Most people stop there. You must take it all the way and put your courage into action. That's when the electricity flows. You can make the decision, which is a plug attached to a cord (I like to think of it as your heart attached to your soul) and the commitment, which is physically plugging it into the wall. However, if you never flip the switch to "on," the light will not work! Your light will not come on, and you will continue year after year to have the same goals. Light up your soul with action. Let that electricity flow through you and all around you. Create the positive energy bubble you want to live in. When you are focused on your future and what you are creating, you won't have time to focus on what isn't working. When you hear the whispers of truth speak to you in the middle of the night about what is best for you, listen to them. Stand up and speak your truth, for yourself first and foremost, and for generations to come. Lead the way as someone who is known for calm strength.

There came a night when we were visiting my husband's aunt and uncle, where I purposely didn't put the butter on the table. It was then that I realized standing in your power doesn't have to be done in defiance and anger. It can be done from love and a non-negotiable posture. When Joe commanded it be put on the table, I simply said, "It's right behind you on the counter," and continued to eat as I lovingly placed my hand of support on my aunt's knee. Surprisingly, he got it and never made mention of it again. Something shifted in my dear aunt that day. She became free and enjoyed a transformational euphoria. She learned how to take a stand for herself, and I witnessed the joy of her happier life.

Taking responsibility for your life elevates your happiness. Always be open to others supporting you with their journeys, but never allow others to control you. As you take a stand for yourself, you will also be taking a stand for others. When you do this, you feel lighter, happier, empowered, and ready to take on the world. You will achieve more and find yourself fulfilled by it. You will create a bigger impact and add value to this world that may even surprise yourself! You deserve to open the gift of _you_ and then generously share it with the world. Maybe your vision isn't to change the world, but if you are one step ahead of someone else, you bring an impactful value to someone else.

These three things are life-changing when you are about to reset yourself:

1. Decide

2. Commit

3. Flip the switch to on (and take action on your ideas!)

If you've found yourself in an unhealthy and toxic relationship in which you stayed way too long, you get to make changes. Let your someday be today. If you know there is more for you than what you are currently doing, grab ahold of your bold to take those first steps. Truth — we all have another next level in us, another notch. I teach a course, "Pivoting to the Next Level," that is self-paced for you, or you can join our live training in a small, uplifting community weekly. We respect each other, listen to understand, support, and offer encouragement and ideas to build businesses together. We take vacations and retreats together. We are not only living in juicy, joyful energy, we are swimming in it.

"Your setbacks are designed to let you experience your comebacks." Feel yourself breathing in a new energy and stepping forward in love. It is self-love that you get to know intimately. We love quotes from others to inspire us and often share them widely. I encourage you to take a stab at also making your own. Dig deep and speak your truth from within.

> *"Know what is important to you and why it matters to you,*
> *and then take a stand for yourself and own your life,*
> *allowing the richness of every experience to create your best life."*
>
> —Margie Dunki-Jacobs

I am committed and passionate to helping others take a stand for themselves, so they own their lives and create the life of their dreams. Imagine putting joy in each day and having the freedom to live this life as you wish so that you can do whatever you want, with whomever you want, and whenever you want. I've spent a lot of energy trying to figure things out on my own, which I found to be frustrating and draining. That's why I'm committed to helping as many people as I can shortcut the road to success and get there faster. I want you to be enjoying it now, getting off the struggle bus, and living the life you were meant to live! Who you are in the moment is not all that you can be. Your best life is not someday. It's today!

Love to you.

Margie

Margie Dunki-Jacobs

"Know what is important to you and why it matters to you, and then take a stand for yourself and own your life, allowing the richness of every experience to create your best life."

When Margie Dunki-Jacobs worked in corporate America, the legal profession, hospitality, and academia world, she discovered her greatest lessons outside of her college degree. It was how to connect with people through one-on-one conversations and understand them at a deeper level. She has witnessed a common bond among us all, "we want to enjoy this life we've been given and have the freedom to do so, to do whatever we want, with whomever we want, whenever we want and have the means to do so."

After her daughters graduated from college, she graduated into a new chapter of life as an inspirational speaker, author, and business success coach. She also founded her empowerment company, Breathing Forward. In addition to her empowerment retreats and coaching, she's built a network marketing business on the Number 1 income earning team in her health and wellness company. In 2020, Margie partnered as a CEO partner with the Award-Winning 7 Figures Funding company to help entrepreneurs secure working capital at 0% financing.

Margie is passionate about her active "In the Spirit of Excellence" Speaking Tour, which she is excited to continue until she has boldly poured into the hearts of people all around the world a message of hope, empowerment, belief, and resilience in what's possible for their lives, no matter what their circumstances are.

In her spare time, Margie loves packing up food and supplies and sending them to people who need it the most. She welcomes fun times with family and friends and a daily morning hike with her husband and two dogs to ground her to show up as the best version of herself for others.

Margie Dunki-Jacobs
Breathing Forward, LLC
Charlotte, NC
802-238-5939
Margie@MargieDunki.com
https://MargieDunki.com
https://TalkWithMargie.com

Living With More Confidence

A guide to help you annihilate limiting beliefs and thrive as a more confident, happier you.

https://bit.ly/MargiesVoicesofTruthFreeGift

Karen D. Haggerty

Find Your Authenticity for Personal or Business Success

I was hiding in plain sight! In corporate America, I chose to be THAT girl. The one who was the life of the party, at company events, the one with the big smile, and the one that never let them see me sweat or stress. I could fit into almost any situation with ease and became so good at it that I no longer had any clue as to who I really was. Shy, I'm not — a little bit of an introvert, maybe. Quiet, I'm not. Bold, extroverted, and a bit sassy, most likely. Am I really any of these descriptors?

Believe it or not, people have a life-long fear of being seen. The possibility of not measuring up or being flawed — even considered imperfect. Does this sound like you? It was me for a long time.

Strangely enough, working in corporate America as a sales and marketing professional, hiding in plain sight is easily done. I believed in arriving early and staying late, which was a plus for getting noticed. Initially, I chose my conversations carefully with certain individuals, who might consider me too aggressive because my voice is heavy and — as some have suggested — better suited for radio. So, I learned how to speak at a higher pitch, hoping it was a softer tone and not too intimidating. This seemed to work effectively, but this situational inauthenticity took a toll on me.

American life offers the opportunity for unimaginable success. It also includes stresses to conform, act and look a certain way, and be part of the in-crowd or beautiful people. If you do not conform, then you're considered different or an outsider.

For those of us that decide to hide in plain sight, suppressing who we really are can cause a level of pressure or pain that you could never imagine! Have you heard the expression: "stress can kill you?" I know that all too well! Let's consider how it affects you. It can cause you to lose sleep, anxiety, paranoia, excessive drinking, loneliness, fatigue, and even effects your work performance. These are just a few!

Case in point. I have a flair for fashion. However, early in my corporate career, I chose to mimic my female supervisor, who always wore earth-tone suits with bow ties. (Ugh — this was de-riguer in the '80s.) I worked tirelessly in my position, which was an inside sales position. She recognized my work ethic but also commented on my style of dress. I hated the look, but I was so caught up that I didn't realize how much stress it caused me. I did get promoted to a high-level marketing position, but at what cost?

In my last corporate position, working in the healthcare industry for a Fortune 50 company, I achieved the highest honor — "Presidents Club," which is the top 5% in your division or company. In this position, I worked with physicians in a specialty field. So, I read numerous clinical studies and learned just how arrogant some of them could be. Consequently, I adapted to each physician's personality to convince them to purchase the medical equipment I represented. As is customary, I entertained the physicians — with great success, I might add — and my direct report still suggested my sales would be even higher if I entertained the physicians in the same manner as he. It was a great deal of pressure, but it all worked well for me. I also loved how the company rolled out the red carpet for us, when we achieved a high level of recognition (highest sales, etc.). The trips, the awards, and the bonuses, I wanted to always be spoiled like this!!! Once again, at what cost?

It was at a huge cost to my health! Years into my corporate career — in fact, a turning point in my career — I came down with a mysterious illness, had a temperature of 103, and ended up in the ER. They couldn't regulate my temperature, and there seemed to be a problem with my kidney function. I remained in the hospital — a teaching hospital — for five days. Because of the high temperature, blood draws, and too many inconclusive scans and tests to enumerate to you, I had a couple of very painful spinal taps. There was all the poking and prodding, and the hourly nurse checks. Not knowing exactly what was wrong with me, was quite scary. The doctors couldn't figure it out either. Therefore, they sent me home with only an antibiotic prescription.

Within seventy-two hours, I was back in the ER with a temperature of 104. I was mortified that I would not leave alive this time! The cycle began again, with consults from every department at the hospital. I was exhausted from not knowing and being afraid! What was even worse were the weekends because it was lonely. If you didn't know, most patients have few to no visitors on the weekend because people have responsibilities outside of you. It's their opportunity to attend to them. From my hospital bed, I started handling business as well. The business of making some changes in my life — if I got out of there alive! What did I do wrong? Why was this happening to me? Those weekends were brutal. Although the doctors weren't clear on either my diagnosis or prognosis, I was clear on the fact that I needed to change some things in my life. This was a wake-up call! I started questioning how I was living my personal life and my career moves. Through some introspection, I came to realize I loved the perks but not the job so much! I also realized that working in corporate America, there was too much pressure and stress to be present as someone other than myself.

Quiet time will also help you realize some things about yourself that you didn't know. While in the hospital, I stopped feeling sorry for myself. I began to use my downtime wisely. I wrote a business plan and studied for a certification in branding and digital marketing, which was completed after my release from the hospital. These were all promising milestones. But the unsettling part was the doctors pumping me up with Prednisone (an anti-inflammatory) and not identifying what was wrong, except that my immune system was overreactive, then sending me home again. In the end, they diagnosed me with an immune condition that may manifest itself as something identifiable one day that could be life-threatening. Remember, *"stress can kill you!"* That's when I decided to leave my cushy career in corporate America and begin my entrepreneurial journey. I already had connections in the healthcare and retail industry, which made for a smoother transition than most in the start-up phase.

Beginning at a young age, I've traveled extensively and experienced different cultures. Insights from traveling has informed my approach to marketing — connecting clients to brands. I started creating experiences for friends and colleagues. It couldn't just be a birthday party, anniversary, or retirement party. I created experiences, and people raved about them. I started receiving requests to help colleagues with brand concepts and brand experiences. Subsequently, I founded an experiential marketing agency to help clients bring their brand message to life through live, virtual, and hybrid experiences. When we consult with a client, we listen to their story, then strategize and help them discover their dream client, how to attract them and connect their brand to the ideal customer. The result is more leads, higher brand visibility and an increase in revenue. This shift in my life happened after I became more authentic!

I'd been hiding in plain sight for so long that I wasn't in touch with my true self. While I was in the hospital for almost two months, I finally took the time to understand the importance of authenticity, both personally and professionally. Although I've overcome these issues, from time to time, I wondered if I were more authentic as a female entrepreneur whether my customer base and revenues would be different, possibly even higher. It turns out, being true to myself and building relationships and trust with my clients has been a healthier and more authentic way to create a successful business.

A 2008 study in the Journal of Counseling Psychology shows that people who are authentic tend to be happier and have higher self-esteem. Ralph Waldo

Emerson said, "To be yourself in a world that is constantly trying to make you something else is the greatest accomplishment."

Authenticity is about honesty and a strong will to achieve a more satisfying life. To help find your authenticity, I've created an A-U-T-H-E-N-T-I-C acronym:

Assess where you've been and how you move forward

Understand and be accepting of who you are

Tolerance of self and others

Habits are fundamental

Explore your beliefs and value system

Negotiate your shortcomings relative to your values

Time is necessary to make the adjustments

Invest in self

Courage to persevere

It's a process that takes some time but is worth the journey and can ultimately be quite rewarding!

From my personal journey, I created a five-step strategy to help potential clients become successful at generating more leads, brand visibility, and higher revenues in their business. Those steps are:

1. Find Your Authentic Self

2. Identify Your Unique Expertise

3. Identify Your Dream Client.

4. Attract Your Dream Client

5. Connect the Client's Brand to the Customer

Here Are Two Success in Which Authenticity Was a Contributing Factor:

Success Story 1

One of my clients distributed frozen goods through a gourmet grocery store but had a challenge with limited brand awareness for her products. We helped to develop her unique expertise with cooking the greens, which produced a flavorful and healthy product without meat. It was good enough for both meat lovers and vegetarians! We implemented a cooking experience and cook-off for local chefs to create more brand awareness for her product, and it received radio coverage. Due to targeted marketing, customer engagement, creating ambassadorship, and improved product placement at the gourmet grocery store, we improved her market share by 5%.

Success Story 2

Another client's challenge was a lack of brand visibility for her skincare company. The products were of high quality, had attractive packaging and appealing fragrances. What the brand needed was a dream client archetype. We developed it and implemented a product launch at a national retail chain. To create customer engagement, there was in-store sampling, contests, giveaways, and skincare demonstrations. Due to identifying the target audience, customer engagement, creating ambassadors for her brand, and repeat customers, the brand improved by 15%.

Summary

Through the years, there have been serious life lessons personally and professionally for me. Most significant was finding my authentic self and re-discovering the REAL me. It also took time to be comfortable with authenticity and know that it would be reflected positively through my brand and me. For instance, my choices might affect my business, so I learned that "No" is a complete sentence. If I'm constantly doing things I don't want to do, then I'm not living in my truth, and it might cause stress or anxiety. I've since incorporated "No" into different areas of my life.

I am no longer the chameleon and have embraced a modicum of non-conformity. I have also learned how to manage my overactive immune system with less medication. Living a more authentic life has been refreshing and has added more value to my personal life and business success. I am truly thankful for the experiences because it helped me realize that I am a conduit to help people in business become enlightened, understand how to authentically attract their dream clients, gain higher visibility, and increase their revenues.

My journey has led me to this motto, *"less stress, more success!"*

Karen D. Haggerty

Karen is CEO of an experiential marketing agency with over 30 years in consultative sales, event management, and marketing experience. She has marketed and sold over $20 million in products and services. During her sales career, while working for world-leading pharmaceutical companies, she achieved the highest level of recognition — "President's Club." She currently works with small businesses, corporations, and non-profit organizations. Karen also produces retreats and summits to empower and support women of all ethnicities, from around the world, to have her authentic voice be heard personally or for business. She believes in giving back to the community and mentors teenage girls to help them realize their dreams.

She also attended Barbizon Modeling School and, while modeling, became the representative for Seventeen Magazine. Subsequently, Karen competed and was a finalist in the 1978 Miss Central Illinois Pageant. She earned a Bachelor of Science in Business and certification in branding and digital marketing. She is currently pursuing an MBA.

Karen D. Haggerty

Creneau, an Experiential Marketing Agency

1341 W. Fullerton Avenue, Suite 334

Chicago, IL 60614

312-520-3017

KDHaggerty@CreneauMarketing.com

www.CreneauMarketing.com

Attracting Your Dream Client Archetype

Ready to authentically attract your dream client?

Discover the characteristics of your dream client to create meaningful connections and convert more prospects to customers. Your business's big, bright transformation starts… now!

Scan the QR Code to Take the Quiz and get your download, or visit her website at www.CreneauMarketing.com for a complimentary session.

Pauline Marie Rohdich

Invisible to Invincible

Why did I feel like everything was falling apart while simultaneously coming together?

Fifteen months into our emigration to Australia, things were not going as planned. All of the money we brought with us was vanishing fast, as was my self-worth and confidence. Little did I know that sitting in front of an agent in the local transport and motoring service center that day explaining that we couldn't pay for the minimum six months road tax and insurance on our two cars would be a turning point in my life.

Without lifting her gaze from the form I'd just handed her, she uttered the words, "So you're in hardship." I couldn't decide if she was making a statement or asking me a question. However, I know that I never felt more humiliated or ashamed in my life. It was the last straw, compounded by the fact that I'd just bought our Christmas tree in the charity shop next door.

All my unsatisfactory attempts to build my new coaching business over the previous months had taken a toll on me and our finances. I felt both responsible and powerless to remedy it.

I've always been a "go-getter" from a young age, like when I got myself a job at thirteen, so I could go on the school trip to Italy. However, here, I couldn't get things off the ground no matter what I did. The worst part was how invisible and useless I felt. I knew that I had to make this woman see me for who I was. I, therefore, politely asked her to look at me.

It seemed to jolt her from a trance. At least she was now staring at me.

As tears rolled down my cheeks, I managed to explain how we had moved here from Ireland. We were on the back foot from the get-go, as my husband's job didn't materialize quite like we had hoped, adding in about my mess and frustration.

She excused herself, while wiping a tear from her eye. As I awaited her return, I found myself thinking of people worldwide who were down on their luck, who felt judged, dismissed, misunderstood, and ignored. People, just like me, with good intentions, talents, and passion but without a voice or means to express them.

She eventually returned. She looked timid and informed me that I could pay three months' tax and insurance. At least my son would get to school, and my husband could get to work. It was when she thanked me for drawing her attention to me that I knew I had regained some sense of myself.

I realized I had applied some of the knowledge I'd gleaned over the years. I'd been able to open my spiritual toolbox and find a way to be heard. I was able to see how overcoming these challenges would make me stronger and more resilient. Transforming my fear into something powerful while embracing the uncertainties of my situation to serve my family best became my goal. I knew deep down that my faith and integrity would help me find a way out of this train wreck.

We had walked away from so much, a lifestyle that offered us comfort and many beautiful experiences. The most difficult part was leaving behind our families and friends. Despite the timelapse, the homesickness and loneliness lingered. We didn't tell them of our struggles, because we weren't able to even admit to ourselves that we'd made a poor decision. We feared that the moment we verbalized such an admission, we would be irreversibly defeated.

Our years of hard work had paid off in a successful business, which enabled us to sell it and begin a new adventure in the land Downunder.

On the surface, it looked like everything was well. We lived at the beach in a beautiful spacious property, which we had turned into a home. It was decorated with our many cherished framed photos and furnishings. Our son Finn was in a private school and golfed almost daily. I greeted the day at sunrise, and we enjoyed the entertainment and best restaurants in the area. Enthusiastically, I launched my new business, ready to change the world.

Ironically, given the title of this book, my business was called Advaya. It is the Sanskrit for truth. My passion is to help people see the truth of who they are and live their life from that understanding.

I had some truths to uncover for myself. However, I first had to calm the constant mumblings from my inner critic, who insisted I was not good enough to make it in my new role as a life coach. Thinking this way was unfamiliar to me since I was used to getting what I wanted. Even if I had to wait longer than the average person, this was true.

Following one of many Google searches late at night to fix my situation, I came across celebrity hypnotherapist Marisa Peer. Her approach to helping her clients overcome low self-esteem and feelings of rejection spoke to my soul. She awoke something dormant within me. I remembered what I loved about my work back in Ireland.

Whether I was the policewoman, energy healer, or yoga and meditation teacher, the one thing that was a constant was to elevate people's awareness. This enabled them to see what was possible in their career and life choices. I've always loved to share the importance of doing the inner work, connecting with the eternal aspect of ourselves and the inherent wisdom that lies within.

However, I could see that many people would not move forward in their lives until they let go of their limiting beliefs and the lies they believed about themselves. I knew I had to find a way to train with her. In learning how to liberate others from a mental prison, I knew that I would also free myself. I could see how my highly honed intuition and investigative nature from my police days would come in handy.

Once I decided to do this, a shift began energetically. I had no idea how to make this happen. I just knew I wanted it. Deep down, I believed that this big test was a life lesson for me. Uncovering the truth behind the challenges I was facing would help me learn and grow into a better person and become a better parent, coach, and therapist.

Five months after being classified as someone living in hardship, one morning at 4 am the voice of my soul woke me up and informed me that it was time to go home. Less than three weeks later, we arrived at Dublin airport.

Serendipitously, Marisa Peer added an extra training in London. Thanks to a loan from one of my brothers, ten days after our return, I was on my way to becoming a Rapid Transformational Hypnotherapist.

With a renewed passion and focus, I immersed myself in learning how to regress people to uncover the root cause of their emotional, mental, spiritual, and sometimes physical blockages and transform that story.

I recognized how our conditioning contributed to how we saw ourselves. We often have an inner image that is misaligned with the truth of who we are. I was, therefore, on a mission to bridge my spiritual studies of our soul's mission with how the mind works, to help people lead a rich life filled with meaning and purpose.

I see that humans have several conflicts. First, there is a lack of awareness of our very essence, often influenced by the way our education system portrays both us and God. Many of us have felt suppressed within our religious upbringing, fearing a God depicted as judgmental and vengeful. In my case, I struggled with an inner knowing that God is the creative energy of love and the traditional teaching that incites fear and separation. I understood that we are all expressions of God, or more accurately, we have the potential to be expressions of God, loving, kind and creative.

Second, we limit ourselves by everything we believe, falsely impressed upon our subconscious mind by our conditioning in early childhood. Our beliefs are formed due to our interpretations of events and experiences we had in our young life. Feelings of inadequacy, not being good enough, attractive enough, educated enough, or wealthy consume us, robbing us of our dreams, confidence, and self-worth.

I know how it feels. When I tried to get, my coaching business going in Australia, my feelings of not being good enough surfaced. Childhood memories of being afraid to make mistakes were at the root of my unsuccessful attempts to build a new business in a new country.

Working as a hypnotherapist helped me uncover my own limiting beliefs and realize why what seemed like a catastrophe in my life was one of the great gifts life has given me. They say that contrast is a teacher, and I must agree. In exploring what I didn't want and why things were happening as they were, I found the deeper part of me. I wanted to help people just like me, who knew they could be more but felt unseen and lacked self-belief and direction.

I began to put the puzzle pieces of living a successful life together. I believe that we are meant to live an abundant, prosperous life. First, we need to clear up the lies we've allowed to influence us. We must then believe that we have complete autonomy over our thoughts and circumstances. We can reprogram our minds and retrain our brains to expect to achieve what we desire. We can also choose to disallow external, negative opinions and circumstances to stop us from living our best life and doing what we're born to do.

Isn't it refreshing and reassuring to know that we can change our thinking and, therefore, change our results?

While this is wonderful, if we focus only on our minds and neglect our bodies and spiritual side, we risk living an imbalanced existence. A holistic approach to our lives is the most sustainable, seeing ourselves as spiritual beings with a physical body and a mind that communicates with the invisible yet tangible universal energy. It offers us the tools to combat stress, increase our confidence and contribute to humanity using our gifts and talents so that everyone wins. When we give, we receive. This is what it means to me to live a successful, empowered life.

Having helped hundreds of clients worldwide understand why they are stuck and unfulfilled using hypnotherapy, I realized they needed another step to living their best lives. They had a fresh start, but many didn't know how to channel this newfound sense of self.

Bob Proctor is one of my favorite teachers helping us reach our potential and live in prosperity, working with the laws of the universe. It seemed the next most natural step for me was to train with him.

I was meditating and practicing gratitude daily. The universe then responded to my inner demands for guidance regarding what was next on my path. Becoming a consultant with the Proctor Gallagher Institute equipped me with a proven success formula called Thinking into Results to walk my clients through a life-changing process and achieve whatever goal they desire. Thanks to implementing Bob's teachings in my own life, I was inspired to create my signature program The Soulful Success Method — From Invisible to Invincible.

Success leaves clues. I have found evidence for myself and my clients.

One client I worked with felt torn between leaving her part-time job and working full time in her business. She was a passionate, ambitious woman with talent but lacked self-belief. Within weeks, she left her job and 5x her income to live her dream life.

Looking back to the empty, scary days in Australia just a couple of years earlier, there was no comparison. Through faith and determination, I went from feeling useless and invisible to feeling purposeful and invincible.

If you feel trapped or stuck in a life you don't enjoy; I'd love to help you. Please don't waste your time trying to figure it out. Getting the life you want doesn't have to be a mystery. Let's do this together.

Pauline Marie Rohdich

Pauline Rohdich is the CEO of Phenomenal Results Ltd., known as The Mindset Detective. She combines her expertise as a Success Mindset Specialist and her investigative skills gleaned from her time as a policewoman to help ambitious women investigate what's holding them back, so they can unlock the power of their minds and start getting what they want. She is the author of two upcoming books, podcast host, and entrepreneur for over twenty years.

She has appeared on Ireland AM, the Elaine Show, and TodayFM. She has also been featured in The Daily Mail and Positive life magazines. Her speaking and client list include Bank of Ireland, AON Insurance Group, and Salesforce. She has studied with successful icons, such as Deepak Chopra, Bob Proctor, Marisa Peer, and Marci Shimoff, to name a few.

All this experience has come together in a way that now serves her clients at the highest level. Pauline believes that getting the life you want doesn't have to be a mystery. Through a unique combination of services that include spiritual success principles, proven practical strategies, and transformational hypnotherapy, she helps women break free from their limiting beliefs and reach their true potential.

Pauline is an avid reader and learner. She loves yoga, walking in nature, and good food. She lives in Galway, Ireland, with her amazing husband Declan, cherished teen son Finn, and their adorable Golden Doodle, Luna.

Pauline Marie Rohdich
Phenomenal Results LTD.
Galway, H65 D542
+353830344121
Pauline@PaulineRohdich.com
TheMindsetDetective.com

Success With Soul
A Meditative Journey with Pauline Rohdich

This powerful hypnotic visualization audio recording will take you on a journey to release your fears and reprogram your mind for success.

When you follow my transformational hypnotic process shared in this recording, your subconscious mind will accept these new powerful suggestions... leaving you feeling more confident and focused on what you want.

Enjoy this powerful meditative journey TODAY and let the transformation begin!

https://TheMindsetDetective.com/free-hypnotic-visualization

Thomas Vallee

Life After Lyme

The Crippling Effects

I remember lying on the kitchen floor, my face pressed against the hard, cold tile. My symptoms had gotten worse. I was at a point where I was ready to abandon that last bit of hope inside of me. I was in excruciating pain from head to toe. I could barely muster the strength to lift my head, let alone move my body. The weight of my neck and head felt like a thousand pounds. I remember feeling so powerless. *I felt like my life was over.*

It feels like yesterday, but it was the fall of 2016 when it all started. I felt like I was experiencing a spell of what I thought was good old-fashioned vertigo. My head was spinning, and I had to brace myself for a potential fall at any moment. I was exhausted from constantly "being on guard." Unfortunately, that wasn't even the worst of it. Little did I know that I was going to spiral down into one of the most traumatic and grueling experiences of my life.

My life was engulfed by confusion and constant fatigue, adding to the anguish of not knowing the unprecedented future. I was experiencing frequent heart palpitations, suffered from extreme insomnia, and woke up soaking wet from night sweats every night. My weight began to plummet at an alarming rate. I saw my muscles deteriorate in front of my eyes. There was no plausible reason for my suffering.

I would get stabbing pains that would travel from one joint to another, shooting deep knife-like sensations into my bones, organs, and tissues. The pain became unbearable, affecting many of the organs in my body and eventually rendered me incapable of functioning throughout the day. At one point, it even started to affect my ability to swallow food. I was also experiencing severe brain fog intertwined with confusion and the absolute inability to complete or even comprehend sentences.

There was so much swelling along the lining of my brain and spinal cord that I couldn't walk more than a few steps without the help of a wheelchair or crutches. To make matters worse, there was no rational diagnosis for my symptoms. I made multiple visits to the doctor and ER, but I was sent home with normal lab test results every time. One doctor concluded that I might have MS or ALS. I could not believe what was happening to me. *I felt so alone.* I didn't know what to do or where to seek help. There was no concrete evidence of what I felt, and the tests came clear every time.

The Unexpected Diagnosis

My symptoms were so severe that I was petrified at this point. The acute pain coupled with no proper diagnosis left me no choice but to resort to self-help. I began to search the internet for any plausible cause for what I felt, while my symptoms worsened each day.

While different doctors proposed their hypotheses, I continued to search for answers. Fortunately, I stumbled upon a story about mold and its effects. Since I had mold in my house, I realized this could be a cause behind my condition. However, as I read further, I learned about Lyme Disease and how strikingly similar the symptoms were to those exposed to mold.

Some of the similar symptoms are:

- Fatigue

- Blurred Vision

- Memory and Concentration Issues

- Disorientation

- Muscle Aches

- Night Sweats

- Joint Pain

I was experiencing an extreme version of each of these symptoms, so it was possible I had either mold illness or Lyme Disease.

Just as I was wondering which of these it could be, it dawned on me. A couple of months earlier, I had pulled a tick off of my back. I was unaware of what this bug was and what germs or viruses it carried. This happens to a lot of people living with Lyme Disease. I remembered I had pulled the tick off my skin, completely unaware of what would follow.

The truth is, that's exactly why Lyme Disease is vastly ignored and undiagnosed. As I read more about it, I realized that my symptoms were exactly what was expected of Lyme Disease. Lyme Disease is transmitted to humans through the bites of infected black-legged ticks. Unfortunately, Lyme Disease often goes undiagnosed since it replicates the symptoms of many other diseases. If you don't know what Lyme Disease is, you will never even consider it a possibility, and that's exactly what happened to me.

Lyme Disease...

- It literally saps your will to live.

- It leaves you debilitated, but that doesn't mean that you'll never feel better.

- It takes away one's physical and mental willpower, rendering one incapable of thinking or performing clearly.

In a desperate search for an answer, I went back to my doctor and had him order a Lyme Disease test through a special lab. After a few days of waiting for the results, my test came back POSITIVE! *I had Lyme Disease and co-infections.*

Unlocking a Holistic Solution for Lyme Disease

After my discovery, everything — the confusion and the disarray —

started to make sense. Lyme Disease makes you profoundly so exhausted and disoriented that you might not even have the capacity to understand what exactly is happening to your health. After learning about Lyme Disease, I knew I had finally found my answer. However, it led me to ask even more pressing questions. *"What would the next step be? Is Lyme even treatable, and if so, how exactly? Will I ever fully recover from this debilitating state?"*

I learned that when one is diagnosed in a timely manner, usually within 1-2 weeks of acquiring the infected tick bite, Lyme Disease can be treated with just a 3-4 week course of oral antibiotics. Many believe it should be an 8-week course. However, I was well beyond that point, so it wasn't a viable treatment plan. I was advised to try intravenous antibiotics, which are administered via a central catheter (PICC line). With this treatment, a port would have been placed into my neck, with a line that would run directly to my heart for months, or possibly even years. The idea of a PICC line was understandably daunting to me, so I resumed my quest for alternate answers and treatment plans.

I dedicated endless nights searching for information, trying to understand what this disease is, and how it impacts our bodies. As I experienced firsthand, Lyme Disease affects your mind, body, and spirit. I believe all three of these things had to be worked on to fully go into remission or recovery.

I wanted to try a more natural and holistic approach to treating this disease. At this point, you may be wondering what that means. One must realize how important, and even mandatory, this approach is to treating Lyme Disease. The idea of treatment with a more natural approach that consisted of healing the body, mind, and spirit together resonated with me more. It simply meant that I had to follow the nutritional protocols outlined to treat this, along with the ability to nourish not just the physical but also the mental and spiritual side of myself.

The truth was that I wanted to regain control over my life. I began working on myself, and my end goal was regaining control of my life. I focused on unlocking a holistic solution through a connection between mind, body, and spirit, natural herb protocols, and detoxing. My story is a true testament to the power of detoxing. With the holistic approach I adopted, I not only overcame the many symptoms of Lyme Disease but also found myself wanting to share my story with others. I want my story to serve as a solution for all those who are battling Lyme Disease.

Road to Recovery

The road to recovery may seem long and intimidating. The truth is that Lyme Disease doesn't disappear overnight. However, this does not mean that one cannot find relief or get better! To further recovery, one will need the right support system. People usually seek this from friends and family. However, unless you've experienced this before, it is hard to relate to what you're feeling or what you are truly going through. I was fortunate enough to have had a good soul, a caring woman who had come into my life who had already been through exactly what I was experiencing. Being able to talk through my pain and experience with her helped me tremendously. It led me to offer my time to help others who need someone to talk to, by giving the support and encouragement you need to battle it out with this disease.

It's good to take a pause, sit back, and analyze your life. There needs to be an active effort to reconsider what you're feeding your body, mind, and soul.

To tread a healing path, it's essential to give your body what it needs. Taking the right supplements and eating healthy food is crucial. Cutting back on wheat, gluten, dairy, sugar, bread, and pasta is very important. After all, healthy food is good medicine along with nutritional supplementation and herbal protocols. Focus on having a well-balanced, nutritional diet. A health-focused lifestyle will bolster the compromised immune system function, which will effectively help catalyze one's recovery.

The problem is that most people don't consider what they are feeding their minds. Food, herbs, and nutritional supplements are simply not enough without the proper mindset. A negative mindset will actually hamper progress, so it's very important to take steps in staying positive actively. It is of utmost importance to work towards a stress-free mind and soul.

Last but not least, you need to try to feed your soul. I know that it's hard, especially with a physically, mentally, and emotionally draining condition like Lyme Disease. Always try to have faith, even when you do not see immediate results. Having faith will help feed your soul.

The road to recovery is different for every person. Sometimes, it's not just one or two things but a combination of things that may work for you. I believe it's best to work with someone who has been through this and has gotten better. I'm just an average guy. If I could do it, I believe that others can too!

Life After Lyme

Many people think "Life after Lyme" is a far-fetched thought, but I am a living testament to the fact that it is possible. Living with Lyme Disease requires a lot more effort and will than just catering to the body with medicine or nutritional supplements. As someone who's been through the worst of it all, I feel the key that is missing in our recovery process is detoxification and healing of the mind and spirit. This includes forgiving others and yourself. It is necessary to let go of past hurt, past trauma, bad thoughts or feelings, and trapped emotions.

I would suggest prayer, some kind of meditation, and a conscious focus on positive affirmations to help relieve stress and also tackle any emotional traumas and things that may be taxing the mind and spirit. Being able to laugh, watch funny movies, listen to success stories, and be around positive people are also good medicine. You will need support. What better support can you get than from someone who's literally been where you currently are and has experienced what you're going through.

While we tend to place too much focus on the body and what medicines we should take, to heal any ailment, you need to also cater to the mental, emotional, and spiritual side of yourself as well. My experience with Lyme and my life after, gives evidence to this statement.

For me, life after Lyme Disease has been good. In fact, I now see this disease as a blessing in disguise that has allowed me to lead a healthier lifestyle and really live life to the fullest. Most importantly, it has helped me heal myself emotionally, physically, and spiritually. I now want to help others do the same. Understanding and coping with this disease isn't easy. I believe that with God, all things are possible. We must move forward with faith, patience, and perseverance. Always remember that in time, you can get better. This is coming straight from a person who has literally been through it all!

I offer my support to all of those who don't know where to start. I also offer support to those who have been treating Lyme Disease for a certain time period and are still not seeing results. Together, we will walk you through what Lyme Disease is and some of the tools available to help with one of the most critical steps, "detox."

The moment you discover yourself or someone you know has Lyme Disease can be overwhelming. It's best to reach out to someone who knows what it's like to be in your shoes. Life after Lyme Disease doesn't mean you're confined to a life sentence. Trust me. I've been there. There was a time I wanted to end my life, thinking I wouldn't get better. However, it is possible, and I want you all to know that with utmost conviction. This is why I encourage people to keep fighting and never give up!

Learn more about the professional protocol that I personally used as well as a personal support program that will help take some of the burdens off of you. My goal is to help those living with Lyme Disease find a way to get back to living a normal, healthy, and happy life. Life after Lyme Disease has helped me realize how important it is to have the right support. You can find the basics — what to eat, what not to eat — a good Lyme literate doctor, and what medicine or supplements to take when you're going through Lyme Disease. However, with all that, you also need emotional support from family, friends, and an excellent mentor to keep your mind positive when you're going through this chronic illness.

Reach out and make this possible for yourself or someone you may know. Let my long road to recovery become the shortcut that leads you back to the path to better health.

If you have recently been diagnosed with Lyme Disease or are tired of trying different methods to get your life back in vain, you can contact me.

Visit www.LymeDiseaseDetox.com to learn more about Lyme Disease.

Thomas Vallee

     Tom has always been a lover of nature and life. He likes to spend most of his time researching about health and dedicates his free time to friends and family. Growing up, Tom was just like most other children his age, but for some reason, he was always a tad more accident-prone. With a passion for adventure coupled with a propensity to take risks, Tom has had his share of ups and downs, achievements, and misfortunes throughout his life. But no matter what life threw at him, he always managed to approach it with a "glass is half full" mindset. He always looked at the positive side of any situation and saw the good in others.

     In 1987, Tom was involved in an auto accident that almost cost him his leg and even his life. The brake pedal cut through his hip, just barely missing the main artery to his heart. Years later, in 2008, Tom suffered a spinal injury that rendered him unable to work in his field. His compassionate and persevering nature became more apparent as he learned to cope and live with continuing chronic and excruciating pain. As if this wasn't enough, in 2016, Tom found himself a victim of Lyme Disease. He felt his entire body and mind slowly waste away in a matter of just a few months.

As a survivor of Lyme Disease, Tom now uses his own experience to spread awareness and help those who are facing similar battles. He is dedicated to helping others find answers and offers one-on-one support to those experiencing physical, mental, or emotional health challenges due to Lyme disease and other chronic conditions.

Tom's tragic story, sweetened by triumph, will touch your heart and open your eyes to the truth about Lyme Disease, which is touted as a "hidden pandemic" today.

Thomas Vallee
R Health Products Co.
115 Hwy 20
Twisp, WA 98856
509 557-3232
Info@RHealthProducts.com
www.LymeDiseaseDetox.com
www.RHealthProducts.com/conditions/lyme-disease

Tom's Essential Tips on Ticks

- How to be aware of and avoid ticks

- What do you do if you have been bitten

- What to do if you're not sure but have many similar symptoms

- Where you can get tested

As a bonus, Tom will share with you three things that anyone can do to improve their health today regardless of who they are.

PLUS+ Find out how you can take our risk-free 30-day challenge and start feeling and seeing relief and results you desire but have not been able to achieve.

www.RHealthProducts.com/life-after-lyme

Tracy Eisenman

Dying to Live My Best Life

It had been two years since my mother packed my three sisters and me into a car and left behind close friends and my dad. My shattered heart, torn into small pieces, was left behind for my best friend Sue and four girlfriends, who held my secrets safely. I found myself stuffed into the suffocating back seat of the overpacked car. I looked out the window through my tear-filled eyes to take a last glimpse of my entire life fading into the distance. I look back one last time my tear-filled eyes meet the saddened eyes of my heartbroken father. It is my last Ohio memory of the man who gave up his college degree to care for me, his first-born daughter. I give him the final piece of my fractured heart. Perhaps it will help to comfort his empty heart.

It had been two years since we moved away from Columbus. I sat on the hot metal bleachers next to the track beside the middle school football field. I was a typical awkward pre-pubescent 14-year-old girl in my Levi's 505 blue jeans and oversized t-shirt on a sweltering 90-degree South Florida day. Fitting in was very important to my self-confidence. As a transplant, I had to find ways to fit in. I found six smart kids in a makeshift book club. They offered me the chance to belong. It did not distract from my friendship with my BFF, Lori. She was not into the book club, which was fine with both of us. The discussion was the book entitled Life After Death. A bead of sweat ran from under my arm down my side. I would finally get a chance to share my secret feelings about life after death. The blisteringly hot benches only added to my discomfort. The conversation began, and my shy personality took over. I recoiled and frantically waited to share with them. I could hardly wait to know about their experience with the light and the tunnel. Surprisingly, they were all saying the same thing. This book is weird. What a nightmare.

It was a defining moment when I realized that my truth stood between my tribe and me. I wanted these new friends, but my truth was my truth. So, I had to speak it. The risk was high. The trade-off was clear. I would lose the chance to fit in.

Stop here and take a moment, breathe and reflect on your own life. Have you ever had to make a trade-off? In my experience, just before an opportunity for growth, you will get to make a choice knowing there will be a trade-off. Your choice or lack of making a choice will play into your self-confidence down the road.

I start to speak in a whisper. "This book, I found to be very interesting," I said, testing to see if anyone was even listening to me talk. Damn, they were listening. I continued, "The light is so bright. You know the one, right?" They looked at me like a deer in headlights. Ugh, my posture softened as I heard myself say the words, it seems normal to me! With those words, I kissed away any chance of ever having a group of friends. The next thing I hear is, "Weirdo!" "What is wrong with you?" and "You are lying!" Through my tears, I watched each of them walk away from me one by one, shaking their heads in disapproval. *Rejection, often the trade-off to live in your truth.*

I peddled furiously on my purple Huffy bike with the banana seat toward the comfort of home. I was bawling my eyes out so hard that snot was coming out of my nose. I could hardly breathe. Mom met me in the house with tissues and washcloth in hand, asking, "Are you ok?" It was my turn to talk. Oh, I am just fine mom. I have no friends, and now I am a weirdo! The tears started to flow again. "You are not a weirdo," she exclaimed. "These kids are not your friends if they call you names." "Yeah, I know, I have no friends," I told her how I knew the light, and they didn't, and... She stopped me in mid-sentence. She gazed lovingly with softened eyes, softly smiled, and said, "I see what has happened here, honey. There is something I need to tell you." Nothing could have prepared me for what I was about to hear.

I was only three years old when it happened to me. Mom was pregnant with my second sister. We were at Grandma's, so mom could take a break. She took comfort in the extra help with two children and one on the way. They were finishing up their coffee when Mom walked into the living room to find my limp body on the cold floor, lips blue, no pulse, and not a breath of air from my nose or mouth. My sister was looking on from the vantage point of her toy-covered playpen. Ruby, the housekeeper, got the car and rushed me to Children's Hospital, while my mother did her best to hold me on her lap with her bulging belly pushing me away and her trembling arms pulling me in tightly. Overwhelmed with grief and distress, she managed to open the car door as the hospital doors burst open and, a nurse hurtled out, grabbed my small lifeless body, and rushed me through the interior doors. It left my mom and Ruby in shock and disbelief. It appeared that my grandmother had called the hospital and alerted them.

It was 20 minutes later when they called my mother into a private room down the hall. The doctor handed my lifeless body to her awaiting arms stating I am sorry, there is nothing more we can do. I cannot imagine the shock and disbelief that she must have felt. During this time, I was experiencing the tunnel and the bright white light. I got to connect with many beings and feel part of it all. I had the clarity of knowing that everything was all right. The truth is that I do not remember this. I simply know it. Ruby grabbed me from my mother's arms and squeezed my leg. I jerked back into the tunnel and pulled back into the vacuum. I settled into my weak body again, and my breath returned. I was alive once again.

Life Looks Different When You Look at It Through Death

Have you ever read the last chapter of a book to see how it ends? For me, death is nothing to fear, so life has more value.

Death brought me fully into life. If you want to live fully, there are three building blocks you must understand how to manage.

The building blocks are time, health, and connection.

1. Make time and use it wisely.

2. Don't let inherited health issues take you down.

3. Build a strong connection with yourself and the universe.

Over the years, I have created a million-dollar business, raised two amazing boys to men, found my soulmate, and have loved working with people as a high-performance coach.

Success can be yours when you know what to do and when to do it.

Going Backward with Bound to Leap

Make time and use it wisely.

The truth is, we are all going to die, end of the story. HOW we live is what matters. You are making your life what it is. Death taught me that I am responsible for my life. Realize that and become more proactive. You can fight this concept and feel disappointed, or you can accept it and enjoy the creation process. When it is working, it feels magical.

My mother did not even know about work-life balance. I watched her struggle emotionally and physically. She was a superwoman. Every day was a challenge with four children, her career, and a house to run. She was always up before the sun, cooked breakfast, made lunches, and got us off to school by 8 am. At 8:30, she went to her real estate office on the prestigious Las Olas Boulevard in downtown Ft. Lauderdale. She was a very successful entrepreneur. She cooked us dinner, coached cheerleading, helped with homework, and cleaned up the kitchen at night. She pushed herself so hard to **"BE PERFECT"** that her body would cramp up at night, and she could not sleep. When I was in the 8th grade, she succumbed to a nervous breakdown. Her adrenal system dived. She got Epstein Barr syndrome and finally cancer. She did not complain. She just turned it all inward and made herself weak. She passed away before her 70th birthday.

Take a minute to look at what you have control over. She might still be alive today if she realized that she did not have to PROVE that she was perfect by being a superwoman. She could have realized that she was already perfect and hired tutors, housekeepers and worked on her sleeping habits.

Looking back at her life helped me to decide that this was not going to be my life story. A proactive lifestyle is just as easy to live as a reactive one. I created my Bound to Leap strategy to accomplish the proactive version that I desired to live. Do you remember the phrase measure twice cut once? Essentially that is what this is all about, except we start with a grand dream. We often forget to dream. Give yourself permission to dream and make it big. We then work backward to create a strategy to find our way to realizing our dream. We get you in line with what you want and build strategies to get you there. Starting with two years from now, what do you want your life to look like? Remember to dream big!!!! We then go through the process of breaking it down first to one year. What must happen one year before you reach your dream? We then go back into the one-year timeline. We break it down into quarters and months and weeks and days. I will share my process with you in a document to make it easier to understand. When you can see the destination and stay on track, you will get where you are going. The trick is not to go off course. There will undoubtedly be challenges and surprises along the way. We plan for that to happen. When you keep the feeling of accomplishment in your heart, even before you get there, the universe will send you assistance in ways you could not imagine. That feels like magic.

The Gift of Health

Don't let inherited health issues take you down.

If I knew then what I know now, perhaps both of my parents would be around to see their grandchildren get married.

What if you knew right now what disease was awaiting you in 10 years? If you knew which habits were bringing it on faster, would you change them? If you could avoid having to deal with a disease, would you add a new habit?

It is now possible to find out what diseases your DNA has in store for you and take measures to prevent it from taking you down. I watched my father's life come to an abrupt halt due to a hereditary disease.

After six long years, he came back into my life. I was in high school. He had worked for his family business during his absence with us, and they had built an empire. My grandfather knew how to run a successful business. In truth, I admired my ancestors on this side. My grandmother was a coach like me. She helped people overcome the challenges of writing stories. She worked on a story you may have heard of, *The Wizard of Oz*. Very cool, if you ask me. My grandfather designed and constructed high-power electric towers and helped to create the 8th wonder of the world. He designed and constructed the electric towers for the Hoover Dam. My father built towers spanning the United States and South America.

Dad built my family a brand new home five miles from where we were living. It was so big that I was embarrassed by it. I got to spend two years with my dad before I left for university life.

In my sophomore year, I got a chilling call. My dad was in the hospital suffering from a brain aneurysm, with a 30% chance of survival and a 7% chance of living a "normal" life. I am happy to say that he beat the odds. However, he was never the same. He could not work after that. The doctor told us that it was a genetic mutation he had his entire life. We can now see our genetic blueprint with a simple saliva test. Everyone has genetic flaws. It is just a matter of time until you discover what yours is. I prefer to be proactive with health matters. Find out what is there and take action before it surprises me. I can help you do the same. See what lurks in the darkness and shine a light upon it.

The Gift of Confidence and Connection

Build a strong connection with yourself and with the universe.

A glimpse of death brings a new awareness of the value of life. When you look into the sky on a clear sunny day, you see no stars, yet you know they are there. Similarly, your busy day makes it hard to realize your brilliance. Take time to be still and quiet. This is where YOUR CLARITY and TRUTH reside. It takes patience to find it. There is a magically connected place here. The chances are that you have experienced this before. You know when you think about someone, and suddenly they call you? It is that magic I am speaking about, and it happens to me every day. Some people call it a coincidence and write it off. I long for this magic. I sit quietly to connect to my truth and the universe. It gives me the feeling of confidence and connection with everything. It is like death. It may not be for you. If you want to see what it is like, I have a short audio experience for you. It guides you to a place deep inside and far away from you. It is a playful place where you can begin to dream for your future.

The truth is that we are more alike than you may think. We will experience death, and death is nothing to be concerned about.

Life is the concern.

Your life is your responsibility. Take it on full out.

It is never too late to create, dream, plan, take action and live a life to die for.

Take time to find Clarity, Truth, Purpose, and your dream.

I live the dream. You can too.

Tracy Eisenman

Tracy Eisenman is the founder of a million-dollar business. She has been an entrepreneur for over 15 years, and runs three successful businesses. She's worked with American Eagle, The Grateful Dead, and coached Veronique Bourbeau to win last year's 444k ultra-marathon race across Malaysia. She was interviewed with Ted Turner and was featured in Seventeen Magazine.

Tracy empowers women-owned businesses and MLM leaders to forecast upcoming challenges, take laser-focused actions and embrace new opportunities resulting in the lifestyle they desire most. Her unique style blends high-performance coaching strategies, modern-day science, and the ancient art of martial arts to help her clients create balance and success in all aspects of their lives. Tracy gives her clients permission to dream big and get the results they dream about.

Tracy holds degrees in biology and chemistry, as well as a certification in performance coaching. She is also a blackbelt in martial arts and ranked in the top 5 in Kumite at a national level.

Tracy Eisenman
Tracylinn
Washington, PA
724-263-0304
TracyEisenman99@gmail.com
www.Tracylinn.com
www.TracyLinn.com/gifts